The Political Economy of Environmental Protectionism

NEW HORIZONS IN ENVIRONMENTAL ECONOMICS

General Editors: Wallace E. Oates, *Professor of Economics, University of Maryland, USA* and Henk Folmer, *Professor of General Economics, Wageningen University and Professor of Environmental Economics, Tilburg University, The Netherlands*

This important series is designed to make a significant contribution to the development of the principles and practices of environmental economics. It includes both theoretical and empirical work. International in scope, it addresses issues of current and future concern in both East and West and in developed and developing countries.

The main purpose of the series is to create a forum for the publication of high quality work and to show how economic analysis can make a contribution to understanding and resolving the environmental problems confronting the world in the twenty-first century.

Recent titles in the series include:

The International Yearbook of Environmental and Resource Economics 2000/2001
A Survey of Current Issues
Edited by Tom Tietenberg and Henk Folmer

Economic Growth and Environmental Policy
A Theoretical Approach
Frank Hettich

Principles of Environmental and Resource Economics
A Guide for Students and Decision-Makers
Second Edition
Edited by Henk Folmer and H. Landis Gabel

Designing International Environmental Agreements
Incentive Compatible Strategies for Cost-Effective Cooperation
Carsten Schmidt

Spatial Environmental and Resource Economics
The Selected Essays of Charles D. Kolstad
Charles D. Kolstad

Economic Theories of International Environmental Cooperation
Carsten Helm

Negotiating Environmental Quality
Policy Implementation in Germany and the United States
Markus A. Lehmann

Game Theory and International Environmental Cooperation
Michael Finus

Sustainable Small-Scale Forestry
Socio-Economic Analysis and Policy
Edited by S.R. Harrison, J.L. Herbohn and K.F. Herbohn

Environmental Economics and Public Policy
Selected Papers of Robert N. Stavins
Robert N. Stavins

The Political Economy of Environmental Protectionism

Achim Körber

Analyst, Deutsche Telekom AG, Germany

NEW HORIZONS IN ENVIRONMENTAL ECONOMICS

Edward Elgar
Cheltenham, UK • Northampton, MA, USA

Published by
Edward Elgar Publishing Limited
Glensanda House
Montpellier Parade
Cheltenham
Glos GL50 1UA
UK

Edward Elgar Publishing, Inc.
136 West Street
Suite 202
Northampton
Massachusetts 01060
USA

HC
79
.E5
K663
2000

A catalogue record for this book
is available from the British Library

Library of Congress Cataloguing in Publication Data

Körber, Achim.
    The political economy of environmental protectionism / Achim Körber
        (New horizons in environmental economics)
    Includes bibliographical references and index.
        1. Environmental policy—Economic aspects. 2. International trade—
    Environmental aspects. 3. Environmental policy—Economic aspects—
    United States. I. Series.

    HC79.E5 K663   2000
    382'.3—dc21   99–049368

ISBN 1 84064 242 4

Printed and bound in Great Britain by Biddles Ltd, *www.biddles.co.uk*

Contents

Figures

Tables

Abbreviations

ASEAN	Association of South East Asian Nations
ATA	American Tunaboat Association
ATSA	American Tuna Sales Association
CAFE	Corporate Automobile Fuel Economy (Standard)
CEO	Chief Executive Officer
CFC	Chlorofluorocarbon
CITES	Convention on International Trade in Endangered Species
CSF	Contest–success function
DSB	Dispute Settlement Body
DUP	Directly unproductive profit-seeking
EEZ	Economic exclusive zone
EII	Earth Island Institute
ETP	Eastern Tropical Pacific Ocean
EU	European Union
FAO	Food and Agriculture Organization
FOC	First-order condition
GATT	General Agreement on Tariffs and Trade
IATTC	Inter-American Tropical Tuna Commission
ICC	Incentive compatibility constraint
ISSCAAP	International Standard Statistic Classification of Aquatic Animals and Plants
ITC	International Trade Commission
ITO	International Trade Organisation
KPS	Kills per set
MEA	Multilateral environmental agreement
MFCMA	Magnuson Fishery Conservation and Management Act
MMPA	Marine Mammal Protection Act
NAFTA	North American Free Trade Agreement
NGO	Non-Governmental Organisation
NMFS	National Marine Fisheries Service
NOAA	National Oceanic and Atmospheric Administration
OECD	Organisation for Economic Co-operation and Development
R&D	Research & development

RF	Reaction function
SOC	Second-order condition
SPFA	South Pacific Fisheries Agency
SWF	Social welfare function
TBT	Technical barriers to trade
TREM	Trade-related environmental measures
VER	Voluntary export restraint
WTO	World Trade Organization
WTP	Western Tropical Pacific Ocean
WWF	World Wide Fund for Nature

Preface

In general, the relationship between trade and the environment is an emotive topic. In particular, ecological protectionism is a controversial issue. While some people fear that environmental regulation might seriously threaten free trade, others argue that free-trade policies are a serious obstacle to effective protection of the environment. Often, almost ideological positions dominate the discussion. This study aims at objectifying controversy on ecological protectionism.

The study was conducted within a research programme on 'Trade and the Environment' in the long-term research programme 178 'Internationalization of the Economy' at the University of Konstanz funded by the Deutsche Forschungsgemeinschaft.

I am very grateful to my supervisor, Professor Heinrich W. Ursprung, for all the stimulating discussions on the topic and his continuous support. He also always encouraged me to present my work at international conferences and to take advantage of a two-month stay in the Economic Research and Analysis Division of the World Trade Organization in 1995 and of an eight-month fellowship at the United Nations University in Tokyo in 1996/97. Thus, I could gather invaluable information for my work and take part in stimulating discussions. Special thanks are also due to Professor Arye L. Hillman from Bar-Ilan University in Ramat Gan who took a lively interest in my work from our first meeting on. He gave me the right hints when I did not know how to proceed and never tired of encouraging me. This study also benefited greatly from discussions with my colleagues and the professors at the faculty in Konstanz, in particular Max Albert, Rolf Bommer, Carsten Hefeker, Martin Kolmar, and Jürgen Meckl. Special thanks are due to Norbert Wunner for his never-ending willingness to discuss my new ideas without ever pointing out that he had a lot to do himself. The tuna–dolphin study benefited from discussions at the United Nations University in Tokyo, in particular with Indra de Soysa. The detailed comments of Professor Michael Rauscher, my external examiner, were very helpful for integrating the different parts of my work and for a different view on some of the problems, and contributed to improving the study.

I also thank Susanne Holder, Ulrike Sachs and Alexander Weisser for their able research assistance. Lisa Green's correction of my English was invaluable when preparing this manuscript and the papers which preceded it.

She never became impatient with me when I placed another 30 pages on her desk.

I am also deeply grateful to my parents who supported the study from the first day and helped me over the years to lay the foundations for it. If, however, my wife, Maren, had not supported me through all the ups and downs which accompany a dissertation, this work would not have been possible and she deserves my deepest gratitude.

Königswinter, Summer 1999

1. Introduction

Within three decades, 'protection of the environment' – as opinion polls show – has advanced from a subject of minor importance to an issue which is regularly named among the ten most significant topics in many industrialised countries. Catastrophes, such as the oil spills of the *Exxon Valdez* in the ecologically sensitive Prince William Sound in Alaska or that of the *Braer* close to the Shetland Islands, further increased public attention. Apart from local and national environmental problems, during the 1980s and the 1990s transboundary pollution and issues of protecting the global commons have become more important. Visible signs are the Earth Summit in Rio de Janeiro in 1992 and the follow-up conferences, the last of which took place in December 1997 in Kyoto,[1] as well as the Montreal Protocol on Substances that Deplete the Ozone Layer, signed by the major emitters of CFCs.

Controversial decisions of the General Agreement on Tariffs and Trade (GATT), which will be analysed in more detail within this study, triggered widespread perception that trade and the environment are antagonistic forces. Hence, the interrelationship between 'trade and the environment' came under public scrutiny. However, Esty (1994, p. 10) notes '[u]nfortunately, trade and environment policy encompasses not a single issue but a multiplicity of related (and unrelated) concerns that have been bundled under the "trade and environment" rubric.'

The relationship between trade policy and environmental policy can be divided into two categories: first, the effect of trade policy (or more general economic policy) on environmental quality regulation and, second, the effect of environmental policy on international trade. The implications of trade policy for environmental regulation have been heatedly discussed, particularly within the context of economic integration.[2] In this respect, the controversy in the United States regarding the North American Free Trade Agreement (NAFTA), which expanded the US–Canadian free trade zone to include Mexico, was very important. For the first time, a free trade agreement was explicitly supplemented by an environmental side agreement.

The emotional discussion on the effects of free trade on the environment can be traced back to two contradictory views. One, for example, put forward by the Organisation for Economic Co-operation and Development (1995a) and the General Agreement on Tariffs and Trade (1992), emphasises that free trade leads to more efficient resource allocation, promotes economic growth and, thus, economic welfare. Since protection of the environment is considered to be, to a certain degree, a luxury good, increasing welfare promotes improvements in the quality of the environment. However, there is also a much more sceptical view of economic integration.[3] It is argued that free trade would prevent countries from internalising environmental costs due to the competitive disadvantage *vis-à-vis* countries which do not care about the social cost of pollution. Consequently, it is feared that environmental regulation would be subject to a 'race to the bottom'. Thus, governments could engage in 'ecological dumping'. This 'characterises a situation in which a government uses lax environmental standards to support domestic firms in international markets. Low emission taxes and pollution-abatement requirements enable these firms to dump their goods into foreign markets at relatively low prices.'[4]

Strategic incentives are also at the core of the second category of interrelationships between trade and the environment, the effects of environmental regulation on trade. This view suggests that countries might use environmental regulation to distort trade by designing environmental regulation in a discriminatory way, disadvantaging imports from abroad.

This misuse of environmental regulation is called ecological or environmental protectionism and is central to this study. Methodologically, the study is closely related to the literature on the political economy of trade protection, which explains, among other things, why we observe so much protectionism, although the overwhelming majority of economists advocate free trade as welfare maximising. Apart from this 'classic' question of international trade policy, it is necessary to investigate which characteristics have made or are likely to make environmental regulation an important protectionist instrument. Which are the features which distinguish environmental protectionism from 'ordinary' protectionism? The answers put forward in this study focus, apart from legal issues originating in the GATT rules, on the political process of environmental decision making. Special attention is paid to a kind of 'irreversibility' of environmental regulation in the sense that one hardly observes environmental standards being abolished once they are introduced. The analysis also focuses on environmentalists as potential coalition partners of 'traditional' interest groups in trade policy formation.

The political economy of ecological protectionism is comprised of many important topics. There are questions concerning the method, applied modelling, and the evaluation of the practical relevance of the theory. It is clearly beyond the scope of a single book to deal with all of the problems which fall into these three broader categories. Instead, from each area, one important topic is chosen and analysed in detail.

This study on the political economy of ecological protectionism focuses particularly on three issues:

First, we will look at what is meant by the abstract notion of 'political process'. Within this study, the most important political economic models will be introduced. The choice of an interest group approach, or more specifically a lobbying approach, will be justified. The contest–success function (CSF), or lobbying function, which determines the probability that certain policy measures are implemented, is crucial for the understanding of the lobbying model. The probability itself depends on the different groups' lobbying contributions. The properties of the CSF have a decisive influence on the results of the model. Hence, understanding its properties is important for interpreting the results.

Second, the focus of this study is on the potential misuse of environmental regulation. This by no means implies that measures to protect the environment have to be interpreted solely as a protectionist device. The safe-guarding of the environment is – without any doubt – one of the most important tasks of any society. However, the desirability of the goal must not prevent a close look at the 'dark side of the force'. This draws the attention first to industry, which can be viewed as a prime suspect with regard to the misuse of environmental regulation. It has been long observed that within sectors, some industries do advocate increasing environmental standards. At a first glance, this would seem to contradict public wisdom that firms will attempt to prevent stricter regulation because of cost-raising factors. However, explanations for more 'environmentally conscious' behaviour are manifold; for example, the marketing power of such an approach is often emphasised. Business ethics can point in a different direction. This study stresses the potential for environmental regulation to be used as a tool to gain a competitive advantage over foreign exporting industries. It relates to the idea of Salop and Scheffman (1983) of raising rivals' costs as a corporate strategy. In their view, it is advantageous for firms to pursue behaviour which might raise their own costs but to a lesser degree than those of competitors. Oster (1982) introduced regulation as a device for raising rivals' costs. Within this study, Oster's idea will be extended to lobbying for stricter environmental standards.

Regulation for protecting the environment contains certain features which distinguish it from other regulation. Most notably, there is a kind of 'irreversibility' of environmental regulation. Furthermore, environmentalist groups are available as potentially powerful allies of the protectionist interest. The term 'irreversibility' of environmental regulation describes the observation that environmental standards once raised, are rarely lowered. The background to this is that, on the one hand, environmental policy attracts a great deal of public attention and to demand a decrease in environmental quality regulation usually implies serious costs in terms of lost reputation. On the other hand, advances in pollution-abatement technologies lead to decreasing costs of abatement, which frequently undermine firms' need to reduce the standards again. The decision is 'final' in the sense that if higher standards are implemented in one period, this decision cannot be contested again while there might be another contest in the following period if the implementation failed. This property of the environmental decision-making process naturally has repercussions for firms' strategies. Of particular interest is the change in firms' strategies over time. Within this analysis, emphasis is also given to the Greens as potential allies of the protectionist interest. How does their influence change the lobbying strategies of the supporters and enemies of tighter environmental regulation?

Third, theoretical analysis of ecological protectionism leads to the question of its practical relevance. Most of the literature on trade and the environment in general, and ecological protectionism in particular, starts with the GATT tuna–dolphin decisions of 1991 and 1994. At the beginning of the 1990s, the US started to embargo tuna products from Mexico and other nations which did not comply with US dolphin-safe regulation. The background is that dolphins and tuna live together in the Eastern Tropical Pacific Ocean (ETP). During the tuna harvest at that time, a very high number of dolphins were killed incidentally. The GATT challenged the US regulation twice. On the one hand, parts of the environmental community view these decisions as proof that free trade and protection of the environment cannot be reconciled. On the other hand, free traders, are of the opinion that these decisions are proof of the abuse of environmental regulation by US protectionist interest. The analysis becomes particularly complicated because, in terms of decreasing the dolphin mortality, the regulation was without doubt a success. The problem is, therefore, whether the US intentionally choose trade-distorting regulation. Or, to phrase it in the terminology of the GATT, was the US regulation the 'least trade distorting measure' at hand to achieve the goal? The analysis put forward in Chapter 5 employs a lobbying approach and thoroughly examines the rent-seeking opportunities of the key players: the tuna canneries, the fishermen and the environmentalists. The results show that US industry largely benefited from the regulation and that certain changes in the US policy coincided with changing interests of the relevant interest groups. Furthermore, the study demonstrates that raising rivals' costs is not a phenomenon which is restricted to foreign rivals but can also be meaningfully applied to domestic competitors.

The Structure of the Study

Chapter 2 reviews the literature on international trade policy which forms the basis of this study. The first main section is concerned with the most important approaches providing a rationale for trade protection. Although this study uses a political economic approach, some commonly used arguments rest on a different perception of the world. Strategic trade policy considerations or infant industry protection turn up so regularly in the debate on trade policy for a lot of countries that they cannot be simply ignored. Chapter 2, therefore, also systematically reviews the explanations of protectionism which rest on models of the political process using the perspective of a benevolent dictator. The criticism of this kind of model provides a clear rationale for the political economic approach which is used throughout this study. Throughout, special attention is given to applications with respect to the environment, such as strategic environmental policy.

The second part of the chapter explains why environmental regulation plays an important role as a potential protectionist instrument. The focus is on the institutional framework of the world trading system with special emphasis on the exemption clauses of Art. XX, GATT and the relevant panel rulings. Special features of environmental decision making are at the centre of the analysis.

Chapter 3 contains a detailed analysis of contest–success functions, a crucial part of lobbying models, which are used to analyse environmental decision making. Special emphasis is given to conditions under which two, one or no players participate in the lobbying contest. These conditions are derived for a fairly general CSF. Afterwards, the results are applied to two well-known functions, the ratio CSF put forward by Tullock (1980) and the difference CSF introduced by Hirshleifer (1989). The last section of Chapter 3 examines whether a regulator interested in maximising the players' lobbying contributions would implement a one-sided or a two-sided lobbying contest.

In Chapter 4, the idea of raising rivals' costs is formalised. Following Hirshleifer (1995), two versions of the model are considered, both of which incorporate the 'irreversibility' property of environmental regulation. In the dichotomous version, the foreign competitor will be excluded from the market if stricter environmental regulation is introduced, while the domestic firm gains a monopoly right. In the continuous case, the foreigner is potentially subject to a less than prohibitive rise in costs. Emphasis is put on those lobbying strategies of the firms which change over time. In the last section, the Greens' influence on environmental regulation is analysed. For this purpose, the decision-making process is modelled more realistically, in the sense that two stages of the political process are considered: the general decision whether or not to introduce an environmental tax and the decision on the design of the tax.

Chapter 5 turns to the tuna–dolphin controversy which generated so much research by raising the question concerning the relationship between free trade and protection of the environment. The case study investigates the political economic background of the US dolphin-safe laws which led to the tuna embargo on Mexico and other countries, thereby causing the tuna–dolphin decision of the GATT. The case study employs an interest group approach and examines the interaction of the key players and their rent-seeking opportunities. Special interest is paid to the most influential actors in the process: canneries, fishermen and environmentalists. This analysis provides possible explanations for the policy reversal of the dolphin-protection laws with respect to tuna fishing at the beginning of the 1990s. It turns out that the facts are consistent with the hypothesis that this legislative change was triggered by the canneries' changing economic interest. This development will in turn be traced back to the changing cost structure of the industry, the new competitive environment in the international market for canned tuna, and biological factors, such as El-Niño, which heavily affected the tuna catch in the Pacific Ocean in the 1980s. Chapter 6 contains the conclusions.

NOTES

1. For more information on the Earth Summit and the follow-up conferences, see United Nations (1997).
2. See, for example, Rauscher (1992).
3. See also Arden-Clarke (1991), Daly (1992), Daly (1995), Goodland and Daly (1996) or Shrybman (1993).
4. Rauscher (1994, p. 823). One of the problems with the concept of ecological dumping is clearly to define 'too-lax environmental standards'. In his article Rauscher (1994, pp. 823–4) gives three definitions of ecological dumping.

2. Explaining Trade Protection and the 'Greening' of Trade Policy Instruments

2.1 INTRODUCTION

Any analysis aiming at explaining the misuse of domestic environmental policies for protective goals has to provide an answer to two basic questions:

First, what is a potential rationale for protectionism? Most economists advocate free trade in order to enhance a country's welfare, even in the case of unilateral trade liberalisation. Why do we observe so much trade protection?

> Perhaps no other area of economics displays such a gap between what policy makers practice and what economists preach as does international trade. The superiority of free trade is one of the profession's most cherished beliefs, yet international trade is rarely free.[1]

Second, given a rationale for protectionism, which protective measures are available, and what influences the choice among them?

The discrepancy between trade economists' advice and the trade policy most countries pursue has long been an area of research.

The political economic approach used in this study is appropriate for explaining protectionism because it does not use the clearly unrealistic assumption of a benevolent dictator. However, the benevolent dictator perspective has been very influential and arguments, such as infant-industry protection or strategic trade policy, still figure prominently in the political decision-making process of a lot of countries. Thus, it is reasonable not to dismiss this school of thought without having briefly summarised its main arguments and having worked out its merits and deficiencies. This is done in section 2.2. The analysis starts with a first-best framework, with the optimum tariff argument. Afterwards, the focus is shifted to a second-best world. Following the introduction of the general concept of second-best welfare theory, the infant-industry argument and strategic trade policy, as two of its main applications, are analysed. Special attention is given to applications with respect to the environment, such as strategic environmental policy.

All the arguments in favour of trade protection mentioned above are theoretically interesting, but unfortunately, as mentioned earlier, rely on clearly unrealistic assumptions. They are based on the perception that decision makers maximise countries' welfare by acting as benevolent dictators.[2] This kind of framework can serve as a useful reference point for policy advice. However, it can hardly describe how most countries form their trade policies. Realistic models are those with politicians maximising their own welfare, or candidates seeking (re-)election. Section 2.3, therefore, lays out the basic idea of the political economic approach to explaining trade policy. Competing political economic models attach different weights to certain features of the political process. Among these approaches, median voter and interest group models and subgroups of both classes are considered in more detail.

Political economic models can provide convincing rationale for protectionism. However, various policy instruments can theoretically provide the same desired level of protection. Why is environmental policy of special importance? The answer put forth in section 2.4 focuses on two main arguments. First, interest groups prefer those measures which have a high probability of being implemented in the political process. To keep the opposition to such measures small, it is important to obfuscate their true intent. Furthermore, the trade-related effects of domestic policies, especially environmental legislation, makes coalitions with non-trade interest groups, for example environmentalists, possible. Second, the choice of policy instruments is institutionally constrained by the world trading system.[3]

2.2 EXPLAINING PROTECTIONISM: THE BENEVOLENT DICTATOR PERSPECTIVE

2.2.1 First-Best Theory: The Optimum Tariff

Under the assumption that politicians act as benevolent dictators, the classical optimum tariff argument is the only rationale for trade protection in a first-best framework.

The argument rests on the idea that a *large* country is able to influence its *terms of trade* by either imposing a tariff on imported goods or a tax on exported goods. Hence, the large country can increase its national income by exploiting its potential monopsony or monopoly power with respect to the rest of the world. In the case of an optimum tariff, the foreign supplier is forced to sell his goods at a lower (pre-tariff) price in the country pursuing the optimum tariff policy than elsewhere. The income of the world as a whole, however, is decreased by an optimum tariff policy.[4]

The practical relevance of this theory is very limited. If the unrealistic setting of a benevolent dictator is accepted for a moment, several criticisms can be made. Graaff (1949) points out that an optimum tariff policy has very high information requirements, because the tariff-seeking authority needs to know the elasticities of the world market. Leaving the world of a 'two-good model', a whole system of optimum tariffs is required unless you restrict the policy to either the main import or export good. Incomplete information on the side of the government might turn out to be a serious problem. 'The main problem with the optimum tariff argument has been perceived to be retaliation by foreign governments.'[5] Both the country pursuing the optimum tariff policy and those which retaliate might lose compared to free trade.[6] Even if one accepts the optimum tariff argument as a rationale for protectionism, it cannot account for the extent of the observed trade protection. By its very nature the optimum tariff argument is a rationale for trade protection, but only applies to countries which are large in the sense that they can influence the terms of trade. In no instance, the argument can be applied as a justification for the protectionist measures frequently taken by countries which are price takers.

2.2.2 Second-Best Theory

This section consists of a short introduction to second-best theory and the nature of possible distortions. This is done in order to analyse which explanations for trade protection the theory of domestic distortions can offer. In two subsections, the two most important applications of second-best theory in the field of international trade, the classical infant-industry argument and strategic trade policy,[7] are discussed in more detail.

In a first-best world optimum tariffs are seen to be the only rationale for protectionism. Taking distortions in factor or goods markets into account can offer different justifications for trade protection in the resulting second-best world. In a distorted economy, the view taken of the policy maker is still that of a benevolent dictator – but he is no longer omnipotent.[8] There are not enough policy instruments available to him – as noted by Johnson (1965) and Bhagwati (1971) – to offset directly the distortions by a tax-cum-subsidy approach.

In the presence of domestic distortions, the role of a piecemeal policy depends on the setting. Lipsey and Lancaster (1956) point out that reducing the degree of distortion does not necessarily imply welfare improvement. Consequently, free trade can either increase or decrease the value of a social welfare function. In the first case there might be a rationale for protectionism. Corden (1984, p. 86) notes that '[m]ost arguments for protection . . . turn out to originate in some market failures in the domestic economy. Some *domestic* divergence between prices and marginal costs, and so on . . .'

Principal contributions with respect to the development of the theory of distortions were made by Haberler (1950), Meade (1955) and Bhagwati and Ramaswami (1963). Three broad classes of distortions can be identified.

First, factor markets cannot function properly as analysed by Batra (1971a), Batra (1971b) and Herberg and Kemp (1971) and Neary (1978). Special attention within this field was given to labour market distortions. Harris and Todaro (1970)[9] developed a model with unemployment in which labour migrates between a rural and an urban sector. Brecher (1974), Schweinberger (1978) and Neary (1978) examined unemployment within a minimum wage setting. The more recent literature focuses on efficiency wages instead of minimum wages in open economies. The effect of free trade in a distorted economy is – as noted earlier – not clear a priori. In models containing efficiency wages, Agell and Lundborg (1995) find a welfare-reducing effect of trade liberalisation. Matusz (1996) derives that the same measure reduces unemployment for all trading partners. Protection of high-wage sectors can be welfare improving according to Matusz (1994) and Bulow and Summers (1986). Albert and Meckl (1997) can derive these results in a single framework and obtain, additionally, results, for example, with respect to migration of labour.[10]

Second, goods markets can be distorted. The main phenomena analysed in this context are increasing returns to scale. Economies of scale are not usually compatible with perfect competition. Important contributions in this field were made by Melvin and Warne (1973) and Herberg et al. (1982). Helpman (1984) gives a survey of the literature. Strategic trade policy and strategic environmental policy, which also belong to these kind of distortions, are discussed separately in the remainder of this section.

Third, although not mutually exclusive with the preceding types of distortions, 'environmental distortions' should be mentioned. The term describes distortions which are caused by pollution and other environmental problems. The appropriate framework is that of externalities and public goods. Schweinberger (1995), for example, explicitly addresses the trade effects of these problems within a second-best framework.

Infant-industry protection

One of the oldest and most popular considerations in favour of trade protection has been the 'infant-industry' argument. Young industries are helped to develop by protecting them temporarily against foreign competition in order to allow their costs to fall enough to permit them to survive international competition.

As early as the end of the eighteenth century, Hamilton (1791, p. 105–6) at that time US Secretary of the Treasury, noted in his 'Report on Manufactures' to the House of Representatives that to maintain, between the recent establishments of one country, and the long-matured establishments of another country, a competition upon equal term . . . is, in most cases, impracticable. The disparity . . . must necessarily be so considerable, as to forbid a successful rivalship, without the extraordinary aid and protection of government.

Mill (1848, p. 487) acknowledging infant-industry protection as the only justification for a deviation from free trade, stresses that 'protecting duties can be defensible . . . when they are imposed temporarily (especially in a young and rising nation) in hopes of naturalising a foreign industry'. The argument was also further elaborated by List (1841).

The 'classic' infant-industry argument rests on the observation that the unit costs of production in newly established industries are often initially above the selling price. Later, the unit costs fall allowing firms to recoup the losses made in the first periods. However, as Meade (1955) pointed out, this argument is insufficient justification for temporary protection. With the prospect of sufficiently high profits in later periods, firms would be able to raise sufficient funds on the capital market to survive the early periods. Only with imperfect factor markets – in this case imperfect capital markets – would there be a rationale for government intervention. This makes it clear that arguments in favour of infant-industry protection belong to the realm of second-best theory.

In this second-best world, another argument in favour of infant-industry protection rests with the entrepreneurs' problems in appropriating the profits associated with their efforts and discovering the best way to organise production. The positive externality they generate to other firms might lead to an underinvestment in this socially desirable knowledge. Kemp (1960) stresses the importance of learning in infant industries. Firms may invest too little in on-the-job training of their workers if they could easily leave and take their skills to a competitor.

The criticism of the infant-industry argument has two dimensions. The first is concerned with the fact that infant-industry protection does not directly aim at a source of distortion. In distorted capital markets, for example, measures to improve these markets might be a better policy. Furthermore, Baldwin (1969) stresses that some policies are not even necessary or do not solve the problem. In the case of training on-the-job he argues that, under certain assumptions, a socially optimal level of training will be achieved anyway because the workers would finance it themselves. Baldwin (1969, p. 304) argues that '[w]hat is required to handle the specific problems of infant-industry is a much more direct and selective policy measure than non-discriminatory duties'. However, although these arguments raise important questions, it should be noted that the main concern is that no first-best policy is pursued. To a certain degree, this disregards the second-best nature of the problem. In a framework in which not all distortions can be completely removed, it is *a priori* not clear whether the introduction of tariffs is welfare improving or decreasing.[11]

The second line of argument is a political economic one. The perspective of the infant-industry argument – as for the rest of second-best theory – is that of a benevolent dictator maximising a social welfare function. In a more realistic political framework, the 'immortality' of tariffs turns out to be a major problem for the argument. But the essence of the infant-industry argument is that of temporary protection for newly established industries. The rents created by tariffs or other protectionist measures are usually fiercely defended by their beneficiaries. Hence, the impossibility of removing this protection in a lot of cases casts serious doubts on the infant-industry argument as a major rationale for protectionism. Furthermore, the prospect of potentially unlimited protection prevents a lot of infant industries from becoming mature at all. Consequently, with these arguments in mind, it is doubtful whether infant-industry protection in practice is really able to lead to improvements in national welfare.

Additionally, the empirical results on infant-industry protection are mixed. Most studies do not support a welfare-improving effect of the protective measures. Krueger and Tuncer (1982) test data from Turkey in the period from 1963–76 and cannot find that protected industries experienced a faster increase in output per unit input than unprotected industries. In a comment on Krueger and Tuncer (1982), Harrison (1994) found with their data set a slightly higher rate of return in protected industries than in traditional industries. Krueger and Tuncer (1994) replied that the welfare loss in the traditional industries could never be justified by the slightly higher growth in the protected economic sectors. Head (1994), examining an historic example from the American steel rail industry, found a similar result of slight welfare improvement although the argument has to be qualified because the 'infant' American industry had a comparative advantage with respect to its competitors due to its resource endowment. Luzio and Greenstein (1995) analysed the Brazilian microcomputer industry and did not find any benefits from protection.

Strategic trade policy
Given the deficiencies of the 'classic' justifications for trade protection elaborated in the preceding sections, the literature on strategic trade policy[12] seems to offer new perspectives on this issue.

Again, the framework is second best. At the core of the theory is the idea that government intervention might be justified when there are distortions, in this case imperfect competition. Firms working in an imperfectly competitive environment make profits. The literature on strategic trade policy is concerned with the question how and under what conditions can a government shift these rents from foreign to domestic firms by changing the 'rules of the game'. This is essentially a 'beggar-thy-neighbour' policy. The reason for state intervention lies in the government's ability to pre-commit itself. Otherwise, firms would exert market power themselves. From a national perspective, the government is still benevolent as it is trying to maximise the country's social welfare function.

The most influential model in this field was developed by Brander and Spencer (1985).[13] In their partial equilibrium framework two firms (foreign and domestic) compete in a third market.[14] In a two-stage game, the domestic government can set a R&D subsidy in the first stage. Afterwards, both firms simultaneously chose their output. The core of the model is that the government is able to alter the firms' strategic relationship by setting a R&D subsidy. Although the subsidy itself is, from the point of view of national welfare, only a transfer, the domestic firm's gross profits rise. 'The net benefit comes about because the subsidy has the effect of committing the domestic firm to a more aggressive best-response function . . . which in turn induces the foreign firm to produce less.'[15] R&D subsidies have played this prominent role in the literature because – as Brander (1995) points out – they belong to the rare cases in which the World Trade Organization (WTO) rules still allow subsidies. The literature was extended by Bagwell and Staiger (1992), Bagwell and Staiger (1994). Davidson (1984) and Rotemberg and Saloner (1989) introduced dynamics into the one-shot setting of the model.

Although the strategic trade policy literature offers a rationale for deviating from the free-trade paradigm, it has been heavily criticised. Three levels of arguments can be distinguished.

At a first level, Eaton and Grossman (1986) showed that the theoretical results are not robust. This is particularly true for the assumptions about market behaviour. While for Cournot competition it is optimal for both governments to subsidise exports, the results are reversed for Bertrand competition. Furthermore, with more than one firm in each country both governments face another problem. In addition to implementing strategic trade policy, the government now has to deal with firms which – from the point of view of national welfare – invest too much in capacity, produce too many goods for export and charge too low prices. 'This is because each competes with the others for market share, whereas the aggregate welfare . . . (of the country) is at a maximum when they coordinate their actions'.[16] Even if initially there was just one firm in each country, free entry – as pointed out by Horstmann and Markusen (1986) – could dissipate the rents created by aggressive trade policies.

At a second level of critique, it is doubtful whether a government could correctly implement a strategic trade policy. 'These models obviously demand too much of the government'.[17] Even dealing with an industry in isolation, any state intervention would face serious information problems. The regulator would need to have an idea of cost, demand, and the nature of conduct in the industry.[18] For actually implementing strategic trade policies, the information problems would be aggravated because of feedback effects in the whole economy.

The implication of this general equilibrium point is that to pursue a strategic trade policy successfully, a government must not only understand the effects of its policy on the targeted industry, which is difficult enough, but must also understand all the industries in the economy well enough that it can judge that an advantage gained here is worth advantage loss elsewhere.[19]

At a third level, there are doubts about the empirical validity of the trade policy argument. Due to the information problems mentioned above, empirical tests of strategic trade policy are very problematic. Thus, most studies use calibration which uses existing econometric estimates for parameters and allows unobservable parameters to vary.[20] Baldwin and Krugman (1988) presented a study of the 16K RAM market. Due to increasing Japanese efforts to enter this market, the issue got a great deal of attention from US politicians. Baldwin and Krugman (1988) analysed the effects of Japanese protectionist policies on welfare and market outcome.[21] More recently, Krugman and Smith (1994) edited a book with case studies on the issue. The outcome is mixed. However, calibration exercises are not empirical tests, rather, they simply provide some information on the issue which is necessarily imprecise.

Also based on the same basic idea of strategic trade policy, the literature on strategic environmental policy emerged.[22] In this case, the government has the ability to set an environmental policy prior to the firms' production decision. If production involves local pollution which the producers can abate at (convex) total abatement costs, 'Governments act to maximise welfare which equals total revenue minus total social costs (productions costs plus abatement costs plus damage costs)'.[23] At a later stage, firms simultaneously chose their output levels. Barrett (1994), Conrad (1993), Kennedy (1994), Conrad (1996) and Rauscher (1997, chapter 6) used models in which both governments either used emission standards or emission taxes. Ulph (1992) and Ulph (1996) also considered the *choice* of environmental policy instrument. This literature provides a rationale for why governments might want to set environmental standards lower than the socially desirable level. This behaviour can be described as ecological dumping. Rauscher (1994) analyses ecological dumping within a general equilibrium framework.

Models of strategic environmental policy are criticised with almost the same arguments used against the strategic trade policy. Barrett (1994) showed that the critique of Eaton and Grossman (1986) carries over to these models. Bertrand competition, for example, reverses the government's incentive from setting environmental standards too low to setting too tough regulation. Ulph (1994) and Conrad (1996) show that the results derived from a model where emission standards are the same as those from a model with emission taxes. Barrett (1994) also shows that as the number of firms in each country increases, so does the government's incentive to toughen its environmental policy.

2.2.3 Conclusions

The models analysed in the preceding section aimed at providing a justification for protectionism in models which employ the perspective of a benevolent dictator. However, whether this benevolent dictator be omniscient and omnipotent as in the first-best theory or only omniscient as in the second-best theory,[24] the justifications for pursuing a protectionist trade policy are far from convincing. All these models have serious deficiencies. The main weakness of the optimum tariff argument is retaliation. Furthermore, the argument applies only to large countries. The scope of the infant-industry argument is equally limited because we observe protection not only in young but also in mature industries. The obvious problems of removing the temporary protection later, additionally flaws the argument. Strategic trade policy which was, at a certain time, considered to provide the most promising theoretical justification for protectionism is clearly very problematic. The results are not robust, and governments trying to implement such a policy face almost insurmountable information problems.

This analysis does not deny that limited cases of protectionism can be explained with the arguments considered thus far. At the same time, however, models from the perspective of a benevolent dictator do not offer a comprehensive framework to explain the extent of the observed protectionism. This conclusion necessarily draws our attention to alternative models of the political process. The next section will relax the assumption of a benevolent dictator, consequently attributing less 'ideals of the enlightenment' to the policy makers but more to 'ordinary' human desires, such as maximising personal income or ensuring their own re-election.

2.3 EXPLAINING PROTECTIONISM: THE POLITICAL ECONOMIC APPROACH

2.3.1 Introduction

The arguments in favour of trade protection considered so far all crucially depended on the assumption that politicians design their countries' trade policies in order to maximise social welfare. The strong presumption for free trade rests on the Coase theorem. In the absence of transaction costs and clearly defined property rights, there is always a compensation scheme which leaves each group in the economy better off compared to a situation of trade protection. However, in the presence of transaction costs which do not allow recontracting, trade policy always creates gainers and losers who try to influence the political process in their favour.[25]

Models which employ a benevolent dictator's perspective are clearly not able to reflect this essential feature of policy formation. In order to find an explanation for the extent of observed protectionism, the approaches presented in this section focus on modelling the gainers' and losers' influence on trade policy formation.

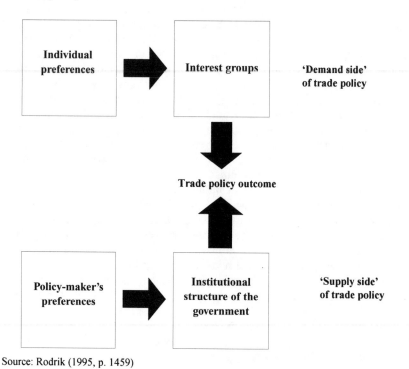

Source: Rodrik (1995, p. 1459)

Figure 2.1 Basic elements of the political process

Figure 2.1 shows the basic ingredients of the political process according to Rodrik (1995, p. 1458).[26] On the supply side, each model must contain a description of the politicians' preferences. Furthermore, the institutional structure of the government must be specified. On the demand side, a description of the individuals' preferences is required and a mechanism must be specified in order for these preferences to be transformed into political outcomes. For lobbying models, this mechanism is analysed in Chapter 3.

Given the complexity of politics, no comprehensive model exists assigning appropriate weight to all parts of the political process. Instead, the models emphasise the different features. Figure 2.2 gives an overview of the different political economic approaches which will be discussed in the following sections. Two basic political economic models can be distinguished by the

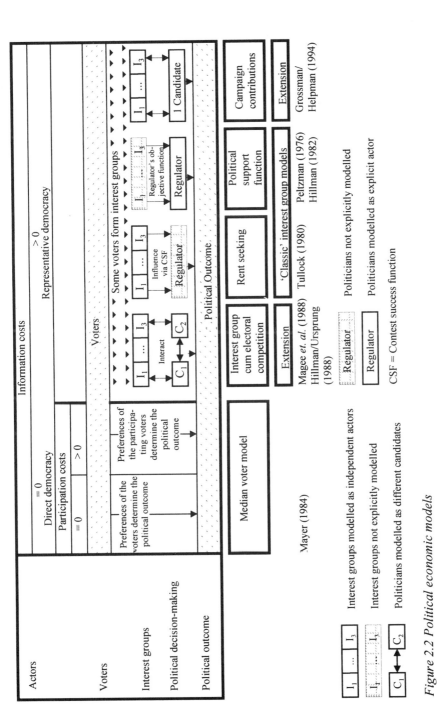

Figure 2.2 Political economic models

absence or presence of positive information costs. In models with well-informed voters,[27] there is no room for an active role of politicians. This fact clearly distinguishes these approaches from the second big group depicted in the figure. Models of a representative government usually assume positive information costs.[28] Voters, therefore, might be rationally uninformed. This gives way to the formation of interest groups.

2.3.2 The Median-Voter Approach

The median-voter approach clearly focuses on the voting mechanism itself. It abstracts from the various transaction costs associated with voting and the collection of information.[29] The theory was put forth by Hotelling (1929) and was further developed by Downs (1957) and Black (1958).[30] With single-peaked preferences of all voters and a single-issue space, the number of votes for the position of the median voter is larger than for any other position. Applying this concept to competition between two candidates clearly leads to the convergence of their policy platforms. The median-voter theory was later generalised; in particular, the assumption of a one-dimensional policy-issue space was relaxed.[31] In this scenario the median voter may still exist but in a multi-dimensional policy space as a 'median in all directions'. However, there are only a few special cases where the theory leads to any predictions.[32] This also means that, as already mentioned, the median-voter model mainly applies to the institutional setting of direct democracies or referenda.

The application of the median-voter approach to international economics was pioneered by Mayer (1984). Building on a Heckscher–Ohlin economy he used a median-voter model to determine the level of tariff protection. He relaxed the dichotomy assumption that the voters are either capital or labour owners by introducing an actor who owns one unit of labour and has a positive claim – which may differ from voter to voter – to the capital stock of the economy.

In the second part of his article, Mayer (1984) extends his analysis to a Ricardo–Viner economy. The result that a relatively small minority of factor owners can succeed in gaining trade protection crucially depends on the assumption of *participation* costs and that there is a significant link between those costs and actual participation in the voting process. Empirical studies by Weck-Hannemann (1992, chapter 6) for Swiss referenda do not support this hypothesis.

Furthermore, the explanatory power of the approach is not convincing due to its limitation to direct democracies or referenda. Direct democracies are few in number and representative democracies do not customarily use referenda for trade policy making.

2.3.3 Interest Group Models

In principle, the policy outcomes under a direct or representative democracy should be the same. Those candidates who represent the preferences of the median voter should win an election and the prospect of re-election should ensure that the candidates, once in office, stick to the policies voted for by the median voter.[33]

In practice, the policy outcome is different. Incumbents are often favoured by entry barriers into the political market. Furthermore, voting for candidates means introducing a multi-dimensional policy space which leads – as noted earlier – to the median in each direction. In addition, the problem of information costs is bigger in a representative democracy than in a direct democratic system because there are politicians as additional intermediaries between the decision process and the voters' preferences.

Politicians, therefore, gain discretionary power and politically contestable rents enter the picture. 'Compared to the spatial models of political competition, the picture has changed dramatically. It is no longer the voter who sits in the driving seat of the political vehicle but the politician and rent-seeking interest groups.'[34] Models of this kind belong to the category of the interest group approach.[35]

Two basic categories of interest group models can be distinguished. On the one hand, there is the political support approach, on the other hand, there are rent-seeking models. Furthermore, there are extensions and models mixing both approaches.

Political-support functions

The first time the interaction between politicians and interest groups was portrayed as politicians maximising support can be found in the seminal work of Stigler (1971). Peltzman (1976) further developed the approach and started to formalise it. The basic idea is that the beneficiaries of a policy measure 'pay' with money or votes. The productivity of money lies in the mitigation of opposition.[36] Hence, in equilibrium, the regulator balances the interests of the winners and losers of the regulation. The outcome is most likely not an 'all or nothing' regulation which completely benefits one group and disadvantages all the others. This distinguishes the approach significantly from capture theories.[37] Hillman (1982) was the first to apply a political support function to trade protection.

> The political-support model of industry regulation views regulated prices as determined in a manner which balances the marginal gain from the political support of industry interests who gain from an increase in industry profits against the marginal loss of political support from consumers confronting prices that have been increased by regulation.[38]

Applications have been made to the sudden change of political support in a collapsing industry by Cassing and Hillman (1985) and the bilateral exchange of trade concessions by Hillman and Moser (1996). Long and Vousden (1991) generalised the approach by making the political support explicitly dependent on the income levels of different groups in a sector-specific economy. Bommer and Schulze (1999) used political support functions to analyse the environmental effects of trade integration through NAFTA and Bommer (1999) examined relocation decisions of firms because of environmental quality.

There are two related criticisms with respect to political support functions. First, the political process is very much like a 'black box' because the properties of the function lack a sound microeconomic foundation.[39] Furthermore, interest groups are not modelled as real economic actors. Instead, the interest groups' political influence can be found in the politicians' objective function.

Rent-seeking models

Rent-seeking models overcome some of the shortcomings of the political support approach. The beginnings of the rent-seeking literature can be traced back to Tullock (1967), who pointed out in a contribution on the social costs of monopolies that these costs are not only – arguing in the traditional diagram – the Harberger triangle but also all resources necessary to capture this rent. Posner (1975) specified the conditions under which the 'Tullock costs' would represent waste due to rent seeking. In parallel, the approach on 'directly unproductive profit-seeking' (DUP) was developed.[40] While the terminology is from Bhagwati (1982), the literature started with Krueger (1974) who was the first to put forward a rent-seeking model, which she applied to the competition for import quotas. She thereby provided the first empirical estimates for rent seeking. The approach was generalised by Bhagwati and Srinivasan (1980). The 'DUP literature' places a strong emphasis on the connection between the theory of the second best and rent seeking. Methodologically, it mainly uses a general equilibrium framework while the 'classic' rent-seeking contributions are predominantly partial equilibrium. Furthermore, the DUP contributions mainly treat lobbying contributions as exogenous.[41] However, both parts of the literature have converged and are now covered by the term 'rent-seeking models'.

At the core of modelling rent-seeking contests[42] is the so-called contest–success function or lobbying function. The contest–success function formalises how lobbying contributions transform into political outcomes. A lobbying function usually determines the probability of implementing a certain policy. Tullock (1980) proposed the ratio between the lobbying contributions in favour and against a certain policy measure as a probability determining mechanism. Hirshleifer (1989) argued in favour of the difference of lobbying contributions for the contest–success function. A more general analysis of lobbying functions is based on Körber and Kolmar (1996) and will be presented in Chapter 3.

Much of the rent-seeking literature is concerned with the question of how much rent is dissipated in the rent-seeking process.[43] The first rent-seeking contributions by Tullock (1967), Posner (1975) and Krueger (1974) focused on the full dissipation of the rent in a competitive environment with a high number of rent seekers.[44] Hillman and Samet (1987) and Hirshleifer and Riley (1978) reached the same results in a perfectly discriminating contest even for a small number of contenders. Risk aversion leading to underdissipation was considered in Hillman and Samet (1987) and Hillman and Riley (1989). Reduced rent dissipation is achieved with certain kinds of asymmetries. Hillman and Riley (1989) introduced a different valuation of the rent; Paul and Wilhite (1994) used different cost structures of the players. Gradstein (1995) points out that rent dissipation is negatively related to the players' strength in the lobbying contest. Ursprung (1990) shows how underdissipation is connected to the public good character of the rent which is politically contested. Appelbaum and Katz (1986) and Wenders (1987) discuss rent dissipation in the presence of rent defending, i.e. avoiding activities. Findlay and Wellisz (1982) apply the rent-seeking approach to tariff formation in a specific-factors setting. In their model, the tariff is a directly linked to the lobbying contributions of the import-competing and the export industry.

The extensions of the rent-seeking literature are numerous. Linster (1993), for example, expanded the rent-seeking models to Stackelberg behaviour.[45] In a series of papers, Magee *et al.* (1989) addressed the endogenous formation of tariffs into rent-seeking models. In interest-group-cum-electoral-competition models, politicians seek office through elections. In order to acquire the necessary resources, they include re-distributional policies in the form of trade restrictions in their policy platforms. The favoured interest in turn supports the politicians with lobbying contributions. The majority of voters are, however, unaware of the consequences of these policies and, hence, the politicians can freely use these resources to influence the voters. The framework was extended by Hillman and Ursprung (1994a) and Ruland and Viaene (1993). Interesting applications of the political economy to environmental decision making were made by Ruland and Viaene (1993), Bartsch *et al.* (1993), and Hillman and Ursprung (1994a).[46]

The 'interest-group-cum-electoral competition' framework by Magee (1988) was criticised by Austen Smith (1991) for the artificial restriction on the two parties' policy platforms of either being in favour of free trade or trade protection. Furthermore, probabilistic voting was used without a proper foundation. The latter point was improved in Mayer and Li (1994) who provide a microfoundation for the probabilistic voting framework.

Grossman and Helpman (1994) extended the basic rent-seeking model via a different route. In their political contributions approach,[47] they neglect the political competition explicitly modelled in the interest-group-cum-electoral competition approach. Instead, there is a single incumbent maximising a weighted sum of total political contributions and aggregate welfare. While in Grossman and Helpman (1994) contributions are made to directly influence the candidate's policy choice, the approach originating from Magee *et al.* (1989) emphasises that the lobbying outlays are used to increase the likelihood that a candidate who has the desired ideology wins. The approach of Grossman and Helpman (1994) is problematic because the contract between the lobby group and the politician will be considered corruption by most legal systems and will, therefore, not be enforceable.

First empirical results by Bronars and Lott (1994), who tested whether retiring congressmen change their voting behaviour in their last year, do not find support for this hypothesis. They interpret this to be an indicator for the view put forward by Magee *et al.* (1989) and Hillman and Ursprung (1994b).[48] McArthur and Marks (1988) found in their analysis of legislative voting in the automobile industry domestic content vote in the US House that 'lame ducks' were less likely to vote for the bill than returnees to Congress.[49]

2.3.4 Conclusions

The last section was concerned with models in which the gainers and losers from trade protection played a decisive role in trade policy formation. The political economic approach provides a convincing explanation for why governments deviate from a free-trade policy. Compared to models using the assumption of a benevolent dictator, the explanatory power of political economic models is not limited to special forms of trade protection, such as the infant-industry argument or optimum tariff policies.

The political economic approach offers a broad variety of models explaining trade protection. Median-voter models are difficult to apply to trade policy formation in representative democracies. Interest group models are better suited for this purpose. In particular, the rent-seeking literature can offer a comprehensive framework for analysing protectionism. The remainder of this chapter is concerned with the choice of protectionist instrument and the special importance of environmental regulation as a trade policy tool.

2.4 PROTECTIONIST MEASURES

2.4.1 Introduction

Theoretically, various policy tools can provide the same desired level of protection. Despite this equivalence, policy makers favour certain instruments. 'New non-tariff barriers'[50] and, prominently, environmental policy are increasingly used as protectionist devices.[51] Which factors determine the choice of the means of protection? It is well-known that in perfectly competitive markets under certainty, every tariff equilibrium can be replicated by a quota. Nevertheless, in reality, we observe a bias towards the use of quotas in comparison to tariffs. If instruments directly aiming at trade policy are available, why use new non-tariff barriers at all? Any discussion, therefore, regarding the choice of protectionist instrument must take into account the differences between these instruments in imperfectly competitive markets under uncertainty. These differences obviously influence the political choice of protectionist instrument.

Apart from the pro-protectionist interest groups' preferences for certain instruments, their choice is constrained by the rules of the World Trade Organization which were tightened in the course of the Uruguay Round.

Both aspects, the protectionist interest groups' preferences and the institutional constraints, are discussed in section 2.4.2 by analysing the most prominent trade policy instruments. This explains the increasing importance of 'new non-tariff barriers'. Section 2.4.3 focuses on ecological protectionism as the single most important 'new non-tariff barrier'.

2.4.2 The Choice among Protectionist Instruments

Interest groups seeking protection try to maximise the probability of implementing the desired regulation. With respect to the choice of the protectionist measure, this means keeping the opposition small and – if possible – pressing for measures which might win the support of non-trade interest in the political process.

Obfuscation and misdirection
In explaining the choice of policy instruments in general, Finger *et al.* (1982) stress the importance of 'misdirection' and 'obfuscation'. Applying this theory to US trade policy, they distinguish between 'high' and 'low' policies. An example for 'high' policies is the decision-making process in Congress. Decision criteria are quite transparent and any industry can present its arguments. Thus, a policy of favouring just one interest group would be very likely to meet strong resistance in Congress. However, some decisions, especially in trade policy, are delegated to an administrative level. In the US, countervailing duties are subject to a petition to the International Trade Commission (ITC) according to the 1974 Trade Act.[52] Finger *et al.* (1982) point out that the voters are misdirected by the fact that the legal purpose of an investigation is described as countering foreign exporters who engage in dumping. The economic function of this regulation – according to Finger *et al.* (1982) – is more to protect domestic producers from 'fair' competition. Obfuscation comes into the political process because such low-track measures are highly technical and less likely than congressional action to attract media attention. 'Thus technical procedures . . . tend to be obscure and the obfuscation they

create allows the government to serve the advantaged interest group without being called to task by the disadvantaged.'[53]

The idea of 'optimal obfuscation'[54] in the policy choice was formalised by Magee (1988). In this model, the politicians balance the gains from obfuscation, less detectable transfers, against the costs from obfuscation, a higher deadweight loss due to more inefficient policy instruments, which results in decreased political support. Environmental policy is an excellent example for misdirection and obfuscation. The public is misdirected by the fact that, officially, the policy is solely targeted at the protection of the environment. The trade links are complex and difficult to assess which makes it hard to qualify such measures as being protectionist.

Institutional constraints

The main institutional framework for trade in goods, and, after the completion of the Uruguay Round, also for trade in services, is the regime of the World Trade Organization.[55] Successive rounds in the framework of the GATT have led to a significant reduction in tariffs.[56] It is one of the GATT principles to restrict the use of quotas and, where possible, to prohibit their use at all. Even agricultural non-tariff trade restrictions, which were prior to the Uruguay Round not part of the GATT system, have to be tariffied. This means that WTO members must convert quotas and other non-tariff barriers into tariffs. This is done in order to pave the way for tariff reduction rounds in the field of agriculture.[57] In addition, the Uruguay Round outlawed Voluntary Export Restraints (VER) and the use of anti-dumping measures was restricted.[58] In addition to the WTO framework, some regional trade agreements such as the EU, NAFTA, Mercosur, and ASEAN use stricter trading rules inside their region.[59]

Tariffs and quotas

The most traditional instruments of trade policy are tariffs. Apart from their protective effects, tariffs traditionally were also a major source of revenue for the governments. In 1821, tariffs contributed to 89 per cent of the US federal government's budget while nowadays the share is below 1 per cent.[60] Quotas are the second 'classic' trade policy instrument, that is quantitative restrictions on imports.[61]

The 'principle of optimal obfuscation' – to use Magee's terminology – clearly applies to the choice between quotas and tariffs. The extent of the redistributive effect of quotas is much harder to detect and, hence, political resistance to it is smaller. The less visible the effect of protection is, the more this enhances the disadvantaged groups' difficulties to organise.[62] Furthermore, obfuscation decreases the probability of retaliation by other countries. In addition, quotas are more popular with companies than tariffs because the revenue of a tariff is, as compared to a quota, not generally assignable to a specific interest group but is going to the treasury. More generally, the firms' profits are higher under a quota system because the domestic firms can appropriate the revenue which would flow to the state under a tariff system.

Nevertheless, as already mentioned above, both the use of quotas and tariffs is limited by GATT rules. One obvious reason for the WTO's prohibition of quotas is that they are opaque. A universal use of tariffs makes the level of trade protection more easily comparable and this in turn helps the system of mutual exchange of trade concession to work. However, it is exactly this success of the GATT/WTO regime which also restricts the use of tariffs. Meanwhile several GATT rounds have led to a considerable decrease in tariff rates. Often, tariffs are no longer high enough to provide the desired level of protection.

This success of the GATT has neither decreased the interest groups' desire for protection nor the governments' willingness to pay attention to the desires of these groups. The logical consequence is a large 'substitution' process of these classic trade policy instruments for new non-tariff barriers.

Voluntary export restraints
For a long time voluntary export restraints were a widely used measure. The domestic government asked the foreign government to restrict the export of certain products. It is possible that the foreign *and* domestic producers gain if the VERs are *truly* voluntary. This means that the 'foreigners' reduction in domestic sales increases foreign profits'.[63] The domestic interests are served by the restriction on imports. In the foreign country, the government intervention can drive the firms closer to a collusive market outcome by overcoming their inherent free-rider problem. This outcome depends on the fact that the VER is truly voluntary. In a lot of cases, it is suspected that the threat of otherwise tougher import restraints by the domestic country led the foreign country to agree to output restraints which would not have been desired by the foreign firms. Otherwise, for a long time this 'voluntariness', in the sense of an absence of obvious import restrictions, made it impossible to fight VER in the dispute settlement system of the GATT. The increasing use of VER convinced the contracting parties of the GATT to outlaw VERs – according to the revised Art. XIII – under the WTO Agreement.

Customs procedures
Sometimes the customs procedures themselves are a barrier to trade. The example of France seeking relief for domestic producers of video recorders is famous. The French government decreed on 8 November 1982 that Japanese video recorders were only to be cleared by the customs office in Poitiers, which was understaffed.[64] The French measure was very short lived. This was partly due to the (intended) visibility of the measure. Many such measures are less visible but, in turn, very persistent. Time-consuming administrative procedures in Japanese harbours, for example, drive up freight costs considerably and thereby constitute a very effective protectionist measure.[65]

New protectionist instruments

The increasing number of constraints on the use of traditional protectionist instruments and their preferred substitutes (e.g. VERs) necessarily draw the attention to the trade-related aspects of other policies, not primarily aiming at trade protection. In particular, these are the trade effects of product-safety regulations, labour standards and last but not least environmental regulation. Although the focus of this study is on the possible misuse of such regulation, demands, for example, for stricter environmental or higher labour standards are by no means solely driven by protectionist motives. However, their trade-distorting effects can be used by interest groups seeking protection from foreign imports. It is not easy to mobilise the public against these effects, because they are regularly perceived as minor side effects of an otherwise desirable policy.

Two ways of using these trade-distorting effects can be distinguished. First, a government can use purely domestic policies which impose higher costs on imports than on domestic goods. Chapter 4, for example, analyses the lobbying efforts of a subgroup of firms to raise domestic environmental standards. Depending on the design of the measure, this can impose higher costs on their foreign or other domestic competitors than those they have to bear themselves. But one might also think of rules concerning public procurement or competition policy.

Second, countries can push for stricter regulation abroad. Bhagwati (1995) identified four factors for demand on the part of the richer countries to impose higher standards on the developing world. (1) Increasing international competition led to greater awareness of different foreign institutions or regulation which might give rise to an unfair advantage. (2) Perceived 'unfairness' due to different standards abroad might lead to demands for protection against 'injury'. (3) Many people, especially in environmentalist groups and labour rights movements, worry about the effect of lower standards abroad on their own standards. In other words, they fear a race to the bottom. (4) There are moral concerns to raise the standards abroad. This applies especially to child and forced labour but also – as already noted in Chapter 1 – to global environmental concerns.[66]

Different standards are by no means a reliable indicator of unfair trading conduct abroad. They might simply reflect the different preferences of countries with respect to, for example, pollution or product safety. The countries might attach different weights to certain dangers. Discussion in rich countries seems to suggest that higher standards are always the best. This view neglects that the different standards might also reflect differences in the countries' endowments or population density. The question, which standards are the 'right' ones, remains open. This disagreement is mirrored by the fact that even 'universal' values, such as human rights which also include basic labour rights, are not undisputed.[67]

Even if one assumes that universally agreed standards, established by multilateral agreements with a high number of member countries, exist, the question remains open whether trade measures are the appropriate instruments for changing standards abroad. Obviously, trade restriction is not usually a first-best instrument. Furthermore, given the limited success in the past of trade sanctions and embargoes[68] leading to political change abroad, it has to be asked under which conditions trade measures are a good idea at all for achieving non-trade goals. However, pressure groups interested in trade protection at least have the chance to influence the choice of instruments to pursue the primary policy goal, and thereby capture groups interested in other domestic policies.

The question of trade and product safety regulations, for example, has long been an area of concern for the GATT/WTO. Frequently, narrowly defined regulations have resulted in strong protectionist instruments. This problem was recognised as such a long time ago. Finally, the Uruguay Round limited the countries' ability to use these technical barriers to trade (TBT).

Anti-dumping measures and trade and competition policy
Among the new non-tariff barriers, anti-dumping measures have always figured quite prominently. They had already been mentioned in the discussion on the obfuscation argument by Finger *et al.* (1982) that a lot of anti-dumping measures in effect are not applied to counteract actual dumping but to restrict foreign imports. Schuknecht (1992) showed how the EU used anti-dumping measures for protectionist purposes. The Organisation for Economic Co-operation and Development (1996a) focuses on the relationship between anti-trust policy and market access. The discussion on protectionist abuse of anti-dumping measures started in the framework of the OECD and meanwhile the WTO has included anti-competitive business practices in order to frustrate market access in its work programme. In the course of the Uruguay Round it became clear that the extensive use of anti-dumping was perceived as a threat to free trade by a lot of countries. The contracting parties decided to clarify Art. VI. Detailed rules were set up on how to construct the 'normal value' of a product against which each potential dumping price was to be compared. Furthermore, the new agreement provides room for consultation. The revision of Art. VI was, of course, a compromise between those countries which advocated a further – almost unlimited – use of anti-dumping and those advocating total prohibition. Without completely losing its potential as a protectionist instrument, anti-dumping lost some of its teeth.

Trade and labour standards
Another aspect which has started to figure prominently on the trade policy agenda is that of 'trade and labour standards'. The issue of labour standards itself is not new. In the first half of the nineteenth century, there were already calls for labour standard legislation although, at that time, free trade was seen

as given and the emphasis was on moral persuasion in order to introduce labour standards.[69] The debate on this issue has been very heated. While some countries want to formally integrate trade and labour standards into the GATT/WTO talks, other countries, among them a lot of developing countries, resist this demand. The developing countries, in particular, fear that such a discussion might lead to a situation where the non-observance of labour standards justifies trade restrictions, for example, minimum wages could be forced on these countries and would reduce their competitiveness.[70] Compared to transborder environmental pollution, the non-observance of labour standards is purely domestic in scope.[71] However, the moral concern is that the violation of labour standards might ad to an 'illegitimate' competitive advantage. Despite these concerns, a recent study by the Organisation for Economic Co-operation and Development (1996b) focusing on core labour standards[72] cannot find that the non-observance of these standards is an important competitive factor.

2.4.3 Ecological Protectionism

Definition and instruments
The increasing use of domestic policies which cause trade effects (trade and labour standards, trade and competition policy, etc.) was triggered by the results of the Uruguay Round, which constrained the popular use of protectionist instruments, such as VERs and anti-dumping measures. Among the domestic policies with trade effects, issues of trade and environment are of special importance for two reasons.

(1) The world trading rules leave room for environmental policy with trade-distorting side effects.

(2) Using environmental regulation, pro-protectionist groups can potentially form a coalition with environmentalists who have gained a lot of influence, particularly in developed countries. Below in this section we examine how the Greens influence the political process and which environmental policy instruments they prefer.

In public discussion, free trade and protection of the environment are often perceived as opposing forces. This is mainly due to the first GATT panel decision on the tuna–dolphin case in 1991. It challenged US regulation for the protection of dolphins in the Eastern Tropical Pacific Ocean (ETP). Two main lines of argument came up in the discussion of this decision. On the one hand, environmentalists claimed that the current GATT/WTO trade regime prevents national governments from implementing sufficient environmental control.[73] On the other hand, free traders argued that environmental regulation might become a threat to world trade by constituting, intentionally or unintentionally, a trade barrier.[74] Chapter 5 analyses the example of the US dolphin-safe laws and shows how both protectionist interests and environmentalists pushed for stricter regulation.

The tuna–dolphin case also illustrates that there is no clear-cut border between protectionism and 'legitimate' regulation for the protection of the environment. '[T]he line between protecting the environment and protectionism of a more familiar kind can . . . indeed be worryingly thin.'[75] It is, therefore, difficult to find an effective definition of, 'environmental', 'green' or 'ecological protectionism.'[76] Laplante and Garbutt (1992, p. 117) employ a very broad definition:

> Environmental protectionism exists when a law, regulation, measure or program is used by a government of a legal jurisdiction to achieve a stated level of environmental quality and from which firms in the given jurisdiction derive a competitive advantage over firms outside the jurisdiction; competitive advantage they would not have derived if another law, regulation, measure or program is used to achieve the same stated level of environmental quality.

This definition also summarises the most important provisions of the GATT/WTO with respect to trade-related environmental measures (TREMs). Under its legal framework, member countries have complete freedom over their internal taxation and regulation (Art. III, II:2(a)). This includes the use of internal, non-discriminatory instruments of environmental policy.[77] However, the chosen instrument has to be 'necessary'[78] in the sense that the least trade distortive instrument has to be chosen. In practice, it is often very hard to find out which policy instruments fulfil this requirement.

Sorsa (1995) identifies three areas where environmental law might be misused in order to pursue protectionist goals: (1) Multilateral environmental agreements (MEAs), (2) Product standards, and (3) Process standards. We will investigate each below.

Multilateral environmental agreements (MEAs) The most important of these agreements which might affect trade are briefly explained.[79] The Convention on International Trade in Endangered Species (CITES) (1973) allowed for the regulation of trade with those species which are or may become threatened by extinction.[80] The Montreal Protocol on Substances that deplete the Ozone Layer (1987) aims at reducing those substances which destroy the ozone layer. It was the first agreement explicitly allowing trade measures against non-parties. It was, therefore, discussed in detail by the WTO. The Basel Convention on the Control of Transboundary Movements of Hazardous Wastes and Their Disposal (1989) was set up to limit the transboundary trade of dangerous wastes. Parties to the agreement may prohibit the importation and disposal of hazardous waste. Member states agree not to allow the exportation of such wastes to countries which explicitly prohibit the import of these substances. Illegal traffic in hazardous waste is also subject to a re-import duty if an illegally exported waste is discovered.

Meanwhile, the Committee on Trade and Environment of the WTO is in the process of clarifying the relationship between MEAs and WTO rules. Although there seems to be a consensus that the use of trade measures against members of the MEA is permissible, the situation is less clear with regard to sanctions against countries which are WTO members but not members of the MEA in question. At the first ministerial conference of the WTO in Singapore, 1996, the ministers decided to further explore these aspects in the Committee on Trade and Environment.[81]

Petersmann (1993) points out that, for conflicts on environmental policy among states, the 'dispute settlement procedures of the General Agreement on Tariffs and Trade (GATT) and the EEC have been used more frequently for the settlement of international environmental disputes . . . than any other international dispute settlement mechanism'.[82] Thus far, no international environmental agreement has been challenged under the General Agreement. The reason might be that the MEAs do not contain automatic sanctions for non-compliance. The decision to impose sanctions requires agreement by a majority of the contracting parties of the MEA. This is a potentially high barrier.

Hence, in comparison to MEAs, the potential for eco-protectionism seems to lie more in national environmental policies as analysed by Hoekman and Leidy (1992) and Hahn (1990).[83]

Product-related measures Sorsa (1995, p. 2) thinks that the fear of eco-protectionism resulting from product standards might be justified because of the sharp increase in product regulation in most industrialised countries.[84] One main potential for an abuse of environmental policy for protectionism seems to be that some national environmental policies impose a different cost burden on foreign and domestic companies.[85] Such regulation need not necessarily be in violation of the national treatment provision of the GATT/WTO regime. The US gas guzzler tax[86] on cars with a low fuel economy standard, for example, was found in conformity with GATT rules. In Europe, it is argued that European exporters of cars are more affected by the tax, because they sell more large cars in the US which naturally have more difficulties in meeting the threshold for the tax.

A second potential instrument are eco-labelling schemes. These are considered to be a promising protectionist instrument because they are legal under the GATT/WTO regime.[87] Trade concerns particularly arise when these labelling schemes include product-related provisions. Such criteria can discriminate against foreign products when they exclusively reflect the environmental preferences of the importing country. However, it is hard to find evidence of discrimination against exporting countries, although a number of eco-labelling schemes contain product provisions.[88]

Process standards   Process standards can take the form of restrictions on the use of certain inputs: water, non-use of CFCs, or the compulsory use of certain production processes, etc. Maloney and McCormick (1982) showed that, under certain assumptions, a cost-increasing process standard in an competitive industry can drive up profits.

Process standards gain special importance if foreign firms have to bear higher costs to comply with standards than their domestic rivals. Process standards might be a source of environmental protectionism if they are applied extra-territorially, in order to raise the environmental standards in other countries. One of the main features of the tuna–dolphin case was that the US regulation, which aimed at 'producing' canned tuna in a dolphin safe manner, was applied *outside* the US Economic exclusive zone (EEZ).[89] This unilateralism offers considerable potential for abuse by setting arbitrary environmental priorities.

Environmental regulation and the world trading system

Generally, the GATT/WTO[90] regime does not interfere with the autonomy of a country to decide on domestic policy, as long as measures being applied are non-discriminatory according to Art. III. This is important because discussions surrounding clashes over trade and the environment suggest that all TREMs are potentially threatened by panel decision. This is not the case because all policies with trade-related effects – including environmental measures – which are designed to be non-discriminatory, are in conformity with a country's obligations under the WTO framework. The Agreement on Technical Barriers to Trade simply requires notifying other contracting parties of technical measures which are likely to have major trade effects.[91] Problems only arise when a WTO member wants to be made exempt from their obligations under the WTO regime for reasons of protecting the environment. In this case, treaties contain exemption clauses. The most important environmental provisions of the WTO regime are discussed in the remainder of this subsection. Central to the analysis is the exemption clause in Art. XX (b) GATT in relation to the Agreement on the Application of Sanitary and Phytosanitary Measures.

The term 'environment' is not explicitly part of the original GATT treaty from 1947.[92] However, Art. XX leaves room for environmental measures which would otherwise be GATT inconsistent. Other exemptions are for example, measures relating to products of prison labour (Art. XX e) or the protection of the public morals (Art. XX a). There are two main exemptions which can be applied to the environment.

- Art. XX (b) covers measures 'necessary to protect human, animal or plant life or health'.
- Art. XX (g) is concerned with measures relating to the 'conservation of exhaustible natural resources if such measures are made effective in conjunction with restrictions on domestic production or consumption'.

The wording of Art. XX seems quite open but GATT panel decisions interpret the article narrowly. So far no panel report found the criteria fulfilled in order to allow a contracting party to the GATT to use the escape clause.[93] In 1982, a panel on the US prohibition on the import of tuna and tuna products from Canada[94] found the US in violation of the provisions of Art. XX (g) because there were no restrictions on domestic production or consumption. In the case of US taxes on petroleum and other environmental taxes,[95] the panel found a violation of the national treatment clause. Another barrier to the application of Art. XX (g) are the requirements that the measures have to be 'necessary' and 'related to conservation'. Both terms were clarified – among other decisions – in the rulings on Canada's restrictions on exports of unprocessed herring and salmon,[96] both tuna–dolphin decisions,[97] and the report on standards for reformulated and conventional gasoline[98] which relates to the Clean Air Act Legislation. The tuna–dolphin panel[99] interpreted 'necessity' in the sense that the US had not exhausted all other measures with respect to the conservation of dolphins. Hence, the panel argued that the 'least trade distortive' measure had to be chosen. However, this is likely to be an empty formula. Environmentalists argued that future panels could always call for a least trade distortive measure and, by this, prevent the implementation of any environmental measure with trade-related effects. The term 'related to the conservation of exhaustible resources' was interpreted in the tuna–dolphins decision in the sense of primarily aiming at the conservation of dolphins, not changing Mexico's environmental policy.

The second important escape clause is Art. XX (b) which relates to the protection of human, plant and animal life and health. The Agreement on the Application of Sanitary and Phytosanitary Measures emphasises that the members have the right to implement such measures based on scientific knowledge as long as they do not discriminate against foreign suppliers (Art. 2.1) even if the measures might exceed the level of sanitary and phytosanitary protection achieved by international agreements (Art. 3.3). The necessity test also applies to Art. XX (b). The Thai cigarette case[100] of 1990 showed the conflict potential of the article. The panel argued that restriction on the importation of foreign cigarettes, while permitting domestic cigarettes, was not necessary to protect citizens' health.[101] More recently, a WTO panel ruled on the complaints of the US against the EC measures concerning meat and meat products (hormones).[102] The EU prohibits the import of meat treated with hormones. Again, the WTO emphasised the right of each member state to impose sanitary and phytosanitary measures. In the case of the EU regulation, the crucial point was that the EU did not base its decision on scientific evidence but on a moral judgement.

The fact that most cases asking for an exemption under Art. XX failed does not mean that TREMs are an inadequate new non-tariff barrier for two reasons.

- First, the cases considered so far were mainly very blunt attempts at protectionism. In the Thai cigarette case,[103] for example, the Thai government imposed restrictions only on foreign tobacco products, but not on the domestic cigarette industry. The panels made it quite clear that just mentioning health or conservation is not reason enough to escape the GATT obligations. Hence, a prerequisite for the successful use of TREMs is that the regulation addresses the health or environmental problem properly. If this is done, Art. XX offers a legal way to escape the GATT obligations. This is important because the use of other legal instruments, which can distort trade, for example, anti-dumping and VERs, was limited by the Uruguay Round.
- Second, there are many issues of trade and the environment beyond the exemptions of Art. XX. Measures which are applied non-discriminatorily are unchallenged because the WTO does not interfere with domestic policies. The 'gaz guzzler' case,[104] which the GATT panel considered to be non-discriminatory, was perceived as a competitive disadvantage by non-US firms. The broad interpretation chosen by the panel leaves much room for GATT-conforming TREMs with serious trade effects.

Environmentalists and the political process

With environmental policies being the chosen instrument for protection, it is not only pressure groups that are interested in TREMs, environmental groups enter the political stage.

During recent decades environmental groups gained a lot of influence, mainly in the developed world. Campaigns by multinational organisations, such as Greenpeace, can seriously influence the political process. In 1995, for example, Greenpeace prevented the sinking of the Royal Dutch Shell oil platform *Brent Spar*.[105] Two important reasons underly this success. First, Greenpeace successfully launched a consumer boycott. Second, the organisation started an influential media campaign accusing Shell of being 'environmentally unconcerned', which damaged Shell's image considerably. The same mechanism applies to political parties. To speak openly against environmental regulation turns out to be politically very risky in a lot of countries. This is especially the case because environmentalist groups are credited with 'purer' concerns than other groups, resulting in high moral authority.

This example illustrates the potential importance of environmentalists in the political process for a lot of countries. Three questions have to be addressed. First, what is the goal of environmentalists, what motivates them, and which kind of policy instruments do they prefer?

Environmentalists' motivation   Roughly three types of environmentalist can be distinguished. First, many groups protest against a certain project in their neighbourhood. Such 'not-in-my-backyard-groups' are very likely to overcome collective action problems because the members are usually directly affected by a certain programme, say the construction site of a potentially very polluting industry.

For other environmentalists – Ursprung (1992) notes – usually the only point which is in favour of forming the interest group is the high visibility of environmental issues. Hillman and Ursprung (1994a) see two different groups of environmentalists: 'Greens' and 'Supergreens'. 'Greens' are mainly concerned with national environmental problems while 'Supergreens' are concerned with environmental problems anywhere in the world.

Of course some environmentalists' engagement can be explained by pecuniary interests. Some hold professional positions in a Non-Governmental Organisation (NGO) and, hence, have an economic interest, in the narrow sense, to engage in environmentalism. Furthermore, the political process increasingly demands the expert knowledge of environmental groups, e.g. in hearings. However, this does not explain the high number of people putting effort into 'green' groups without deriving monetary benefits from it. Hillman and Ursprung (1992) note:

> The supergreen position may be based on self-interest – the supergreen may be concerned with the effect on his or her welfare of the clearing of foreign rainforests because of the implications for photosynthesisation. Or the supergreen position may be motivated by an aesthetic or altruist (or paternalistic) concern regarding environmental consequences of production or consumption activities abroad.[106]

These interests not resting on self-interested motives, however, apply to a lesser degree to the 'green' position.[107] Even without a more detailed analysis of the environmentalists' values and motives it should be noted that a lot of people share the perception of 'Greens' and 'Supergreens' being motivated by purer concerns than self-interest. This moral authority largely contributes to the damage that environmentalists can inflict on the image of certain groups or political parties by attacking them as 'environmentally unconscious'.

Environmentalists usually have two opportunities to influence environmental decision making in their favour. First, they can become a political party. The Green Party in Germany emerged from different environmental movements, among them the anti-nuclear power movement of the 1970s. By entering parliament in a representative democratic system, the environmentalists can try to form a coalition government with other parties in order to pursue their goals. Also, in France, there is a process of environmental movements having transformed into parties, although their strength in parliament is not as big as in Germany.

Second, and more commonly, environmentalists try to influence the policy platforms of already existing parties. They can support candidates who offer the policy platform which comes closest to their opinions. A lot of governments undertake efforts to integrate environmentally concerned NGOs into the political process in order to keep the protest off the streets.

Hood (1995, p. 15) who examines a case study from Canada notes that this process caused an 'increase in the relative and absolute power of environmentalist interest groups . . . There has been an explosion of issue specific and institutionalized interest group activity within the field of environmental policy'.

For any business group seeking trade protection by lobbying for TREMs, the Greens might be a powerful coalition partner. 'Capture' of environmental groups by the protectionists can significantly increase the probability of the success of TREMs. This means that environmentalists might find themselves in strange coalitions, with business or industry groups supporting the same party or candidate. Yandle (1989) speaks of 'bootleggers' and 'baptists'. In his example both groups seek to close corner liquor shops on Sundays. For the bootleggers, it is the chance to sell their alcohol, for the Baptists it is a religious goal. Chapter 4 depicts a coalition of Greens lobbying with an industry group for the introduction of an environmental tax.

Environmentalists' choice of policy instruments   The discussion thus far has it made clear that the 'Greens' and 'Supergreens' might be potentially powerful allies for trade interests depending on the policy instruments the environmentalists prefer.

Hoekman and Leidy (1992) stress that any environmental policy decision has two parts. First, the desired level has to be determined and, second, the means of environmental quality regulation must be decided upon. Naturally, the environmentalists' priority is the first question, while for the industry interest, the second question is of higher importance. Literature building on the insights of Buchanan and Tullock (1975) emphasises that producers prefer a regulatory approach because that leads to cartel-like profits. Maloney and McCormick (1982), Oster (1982) and Salop and Scheffman (1983) emphasise the potential of regulation for discriminating among industry subgroups. Hoekman and Leidy (1992) analyse producers' interests with respect to environmental policies in an open economy. Restrictions on domestic output can benefit firms in a closed economy by combining domestic industry in a cartel leading to corresponding higher profits. In an open economy, however, they lead to increased import demand. In effect, a lot of import competing firms will claim 'injury' and the demand for protection will increase. Process standards lead to the same result when the domestic industry is homogenous. However, process standards are very desirable for domestic producers if foreign firms can be more heavily burdened with the costs.[108] Therefore, domestic producers clearly have an incentive to engage in favour of unique domestic standards.

Usually, environmentalists are considered to have a preference for standard-setting.[109]

> Environmentalists, as a rule, also strongly prefer regulatory instruments. The environmentalists' attitude is usually explained by their inability to accept that the environment, just as any other economic good, has a price . . . Moreover, if one advocates, as the environmentalists usually do, a zero-pollution solution, prohibiting pollution-producing activities is indeed simpler than setting a prohibitive pollution tax rate.[110]

The same pro-regulatory preference attributed to the Greens underlies the model of Hahn (1989), which explains the degree of market orientation of the environmental policies.

Hence, domestic producers and environmentalists are frequently likely to have the same preference for environmental policy instruments. In a lot of cases, both groups prefer the same policy instruments for completely different reasons.[111] Often the green pressure groups are likely to strengthen the industry groups seeking protection with environmental policy instruments. However, the analysis of Chapter 4 shows that, in a two-staged decision process for TREMs, the Greens can still influence the probability of implementing the measure.

2.4.4 Conclusions

In this subsection, those determinants were analysed which have been the driving force of making TREMs an important protectionist instrument. It was argued along two lines. First, pro-protectionist interest groups will prefer instruments which obfuscate the true (protectionist) intent of the measure and which help them find powerful allies. Both are true for TREMs. Since trade effects of environmental legislation are frequently perceived as a side effect of an otherwise desirable policy, resistance against stricter environmental regulation might turn out to be difficult. Furthermore, the emergence of influential Green pressure groups made environmental regulations more interesting for the protectionist groups because the Greens are likely to share their preference for policy instruments. Second, the WTO-Agreement of 1994 further constrains the choice of instruments. VERs and anti-dumping, for example, were outlawed or their use was restricted. TREMs are very appealing to protectionist interest groups because they offer – under certain conditions – a legal way to erect barriers to free trade.

NOTES

1   Rodrik (1995, p. 1458).
2   In a second-best framework, the interpretation of a social welfare function (SWF) is more careful. Dixit (1996, p. 8) states that in a first-best world 'policy was made by an omnipotent, omniscient, and benevolent dictator. The work on second-best removed the

omnipotence'. In line with this argument Drèze and Stern (1987), interpret the SWF as a subjective value judgement of the social planner.

3 If not otherwise indicated, the term 'world trading system' describes the framework of the World Trade Organization (WTO), and, prior to 1994, the countries' obligations under the General Agreement on Tariffs and Trade (GATT).

4 Important contributions to the optimum tariff policy were made by Lerner (1934), Scitovsky (1942), Lerner (1944), Kaldor (1940) and Johnson (1951). The literature was surveyed by Corden (1989).

5 See Hillman (1992, p. 3).

6 Only under restrictive conditions, Johnson (1954) showed for a two-country case that a solution exists in which the country pursuing an optimal tariff policy might win despite retaliation.

7 The answer to the question whether strategic trade policy belongs to the realm of the second-best or the first-best theory is ambiguous. It depends on the existence of domestic distortions within the framework of the model. On the one hand, it can be argued that models of the type introduced by Brander and Spencer (1985) do not contain domestic distortions because consumers are not modelled. On the other hand, by its very nature, strategic trade policy focuses on market imperfections which usually also include domestic distortions. Following this reasoning it can be argued that models of the type of Brander and Spencer (1985) contain a special feature by not explicitly modelling consumers. By this special assumption, an otherwise second-best framework is made first-best and, thus, strategic trade policy should be considered part of the second-best theory. The latter view on strategic trade policy is followed within this study.

8 See Dixit (1996, p. 8).

9 Although it did in itself intend to explain protectionism, the model by Harris and Todaro (1970) for a whole class of models some of which were developed to analyse trade effects. Some of them are cited in the remainder of the section.

10 The 'infant-industry argument', as discussed in the next subsection, also belongs in the realm of distorted factor markets.

11 Dasgupta (1986), for example, constructed a model in which infant-industry protection is welfare improving.

12 For the classification of strategic trade policy as part of the second-best theory see note 7.

13 The first ideas concerning strategic trade policy date back to a series of papers which were written in the beginning of the 1980s, most notably by Dixit and Norman (1980), Lancaster (1980), Krugman (1979), Krugman (1980), Krugman (1981), Helpman (1981) and Ethier (1982). For a survey of the literature, see Maggi (1996).

14 The latter assumption avoids effects on the consumers.

15 Brander (1995, p. 1409).

16 Grossman (1987, p. 55).

17 Rodrik (1993, p. 1).

18 See Brander (1995, p. 1423).

19 Krugman (1987, pp. 140–41). It should be noted that the strategic trade policy models discussed thus far are partial equilibrium and can by nature only deal with an industry in isolation.

20 See Fung (1994, p. 1892).

21 See Brander (1995, p. 1442).

22 For a survey of the literature see Ulph (1994).

23 Ulph (1994, p. 18).

24 See Dixit (1996, p. 8).

25 See Ursprung (1988, p. 31).

26 For an alternative overview see also Hillman (1989, chapter 1).

27 Most models work with the assumption that information for the voters is costless.

28 Models of a representative democracy with zero information costs usually result in the median voter outcome. See Enelow and Hinich (1984).

29   It just assumed that re-contracting costs exist, which make the application of the Coase theorem impossible.
30   The book cited summarises the work of Black published in several papers in the 1940s.
31   For a survey of the early results see Davis *et al.* (1970) and Riker and Ordeshook (1993).
32   For an overview of the spatial theory of voting see Enelow and Hinich (1984).
33   See Hillman (1989, p. 43).
34   Ursprung (1992, p. 11).
35   A survey on the different interest group approaches can be found in Mitchell and Munger (1991).
36   See Peltzman (1976), p. 214).
37   Becker (1976, p. 245) points out that within capture theories 'legislation does not promote "general welfare" because it is "captured" by producers'. For a more detailed discussion of the distinction among capture theories and the approach of Peltzman (1976), see also Becker (1976, pp. 245–46).
38   Hillman (1989, p. 26). According to Grossman and Helpman (1994, p. 833) '[t]he "political-support function" has as arguments the welfare that designated interest groups derive from the chosen policies and the deadweight loss that the policies impose on society at large'.
39   Grossman and Helpman (1995) who derive a kind of political support function from the equilibrium actions of profit-maximising interest groups, constitute an exception. In this paper they further elaborate an idea they put forward in Grossman and Helpman (1994). Yang (1995) is also more explicit on the microeconomic foundation of political support functions.
40   Bhagwati (1982, p. 989) defines 'Directly Unproductive Profit-Seeking' as activities that 'yield pecuniary returns but do not produce goods or services that enter a utility function directly or indirectly via increased production or availability to the economy of goods that enter a utility function. Insofar as such activities use real resources, they result in a contraction of the availability set open to the economy'.
41   For a more detailed discussion of the differences see Rowley (1988).
42   For a survey, see Nitzan (1994).
43   Although the literature on 'rent dissipation' is not directly linked to trade policy formation, a lot of the contributions cited in the remainder of this paragraph are an important theoretical input to the literature on protectionism.
44   For a comprehensive analysis of Tullock's original game see Cleeton (1989) or Perez Castrillo and Verdier (1992).
45   A representative collection of articles can be found in Tollinson and Congleton (1995).
46   For a more detailed analysis of these issues see Chapter 4. For a survey of the literature on trade and the environment, see Schulze and Ursprung (2000).
47   The terminology is due to Rodrik (1995).
48   Grossman and Helpman (1995) placed more weight on the active role of the interest groups. The lobbies, like those in Magee *et al.* (1989), decide on the size of campaign contributions they offer to the political representatives. Unlike the interest group in the interest-group-cum-electoral-competition approach, the lobbies try to influence the policy pronouncements themselves while Magee *et al.* (1989) sees lobbies setting their contributions after the policy pronouncements.
49   See also Stratmann (1991).
50   In the literature, trade protecting measures which are not tariffs or quotas are referred to as either the 'new protectionist instruments' or 'non-tariff barriers'. However, the latter term also includes, by definition, quotas. To avoid problems, in this context non-tariff barriers other than quotas are referred to as 'new non-tariff barriers'.
51   The importance of environmental policies for the world trading system was emphasised by politicians during the ministerial meeting of the WTO in Geneva in April 1998. See for, for example, Clinton (1998, pp. 1–2) which contains the speech of the US president in Geneva. The ministerial declaration also underlined the importance of proceeding with the

agenda of Marrakesh which established – among other things – the Committee on Trade and the Environment. See World Trade Organization (1998a, pp. 1–2).

52   McCubbins and Page (1986) argue that Congress always delegates authority to administrative agencies when there is a lot of conflict and uncertainty. This leads congressmen to enact a lot of procedural safeguards. The agency, evaluated according to its own incentive scheme, has to show some visible signs of accomplishment with respect to the policy goal spelled out by the parliament.

53   Finger *et al.* (1982, p. 454).

54   Hillman (1977) illustrates the influence of obfuscation on the choice of policy instruments with his analysis of the Brigden report of 1929 on the Australian tariff system. The Australian Government, at that time eager to increase the workforce, set up a commission to review the policy of protection of domestic labour-intensive industries. The report makes it clear that the commission was aware of the fact that the goal of increasing the workforce could have been achieved with lower costs by a subsidy than those caused by the tariff. The wording of the report makes it clear that the government knew all this but the politicians chose a tariff in order to obscure the costs.

55   The World Trade Organization (WTO) was founded with the ratification of 'The Final Act Embodying the Results of the Uruguay Round of Multilateral Trade Negotiations', signed on 15 April 1994 in Marrakesh. The GATT Treaty of 1947 governing trade in goods is an integral part of the new treaty. However, the WTO agreement is much more comprehensive than the GATT. It also incorporates all codes of the preceding GATT round, such as the Code on Subsidies of the Tokyo Round which were not signed by all GATT contracting parties. The agreement also includes trade in service, agriculture, phasing out of the multi-fibre agreement, etc. Most of the rules governing the area of trade and the environment already existed in the old GATT. Hence, GATT-, WTO-, or GATT/WTO regime are used as synonyms within this study. If there are changes originating from the WTO agreement, this is indicated separately.

56   The Tokyo Round, for example, decreased the average tariffs on industrial products to 4.7 per cent.

57   The first reduction round is due five years after implementation of the Uruguay Round.

58   Art. VI was amended by definitions, for example, of how to determine whether a product is dumped.

59   This study focuses on those institutional constraints arising from the GATT/WTO regime.

60   However, although the decreasing importance of tariff revenues for the national governments is a general trend, the figures for the US additionally reflect the constitutional constraints on the US federal government's ability to raise other funds.

61   For a theoretical analysis of the choice among tariffs and quotas see, e.g. Cassing and Hillman (1985).

62   See the arguments of Olson (1965) for the organisation of groups.

63   Hillman and Ursprung (1988, p. 738).

64   For more details see *Time* (1982) and Bremer (1992). A lot of newspapers addressed the French measure as a second Battle of Poiters referring to the battle of AD 732 when a Frankish army stopped an attacking Arab army.

65   See, for example, *Handelsblatt* (1997, p. 2).

66   Art. XXe GATT is concerned with prison labour.

67   The discussion on 'Asian Values' shows a lot of the problems with 'universal' values. Do the attacks of some Asian leaders on a kind of 'value imperialism' simply reflect the desire of the ruling class to secure their rents which were potentially threatened or do they legitimately attach different weights to certain values?

68   See, for example, Kaempfer and Lowenberg (1992) and Hufbauer *et al.* (1990).

69   See Hanson (1983).

70   For a more detailed analysis of the possible consequences of harmonising labour standards see Brown *et al.* (1996).

71   See Bhagwati (1995, p. 755).

72   The OECD defines core labour standards as the elimination of child labour exploitation, the prohibition of forced labour, the freedom of association, the right to organise and bargain collectively, and non-discrimination in employment.

73   See Charnovitz (1991), Charnovitz (1992), or Esty (1994).

74   See *Economist* (1993a, p. 15), *Economist* (1993b, p. 19).

75   *Time* (1982, p. 26).

76   All terms will be used synonymously throughout the study.

77   See Petersmann (1995, p. 19).

78   See General Agreement on Tariffs and Trade (1991).

79   There are more than 20 MEAs with trade provisions. Esty (1994, pp. 275–81) gives a brief summary of most of them. For a list of the most important agreements, see also General Agreement on Tariffs and Trade (1992, appendix 1).

80   For a detailed discussion of the trade-related measures incorporated in CITES, see Organisation for Economic Co-operation and Development (1997).

81   See World Trade Organization (1998b, p. 1).

82   Petersmann (1993, p. 43).

83   A series of Hahn's papers on environmental policy from the 1980s is summarised in Hahn (1990).

84   Sorsa (1995) uses the notifications to the GATT Technical Barriers to Trade Code as an indicator.

85   In Chapter 4, it will be demonstrated that lobbying for stricter environmental law cannot only be used to disadvantage foreign competitors but also as a device for intra-industrial competition among different subgroups of the same domestic industry. From a domestic point of view, Buchanan and Tullock (1975) and Maloney and McCormick (1982) show the possibility of domestic industries benefiting from environmental regulation.

86   See General Agreement on Tariffs and Trade (1994b).

87   See General Agreement on Tariffs and Trade (1991).

88   For an analysis of the most prominent eco-labelling schemes world-wide, see Organisation for Economic Co-operation and Development (1995b).

89   For a more detailed discussion of the tuna–dolphin case, see Chapter 5.

90   Again, it has to be noted, that the WTO rules are not the only framework limiting the use of environmental policy measures. Within the EU, for example, decisions of the European Court of Justice were of vital importance for intra-EU trade and partly for trade between the EU and other nations. The most prominent decisions are the Danish Bottle Case and the Cassis Dijon decision which led to the principle of the mutual recognition of standards within the EU. However, analysing the relationship of trading and environmental rules for most of these agreements would be beyond the scope of this study. With 143 members, the WTO rules come closest to universal trading rules, and, hence, the focus is on the WTO regime.

91   In the pre-Uruguay Round only 48 countries were members of the agreement but the Uruguay Round made it part of all WTO members' obligations.

92   Hereafter abbreviated as GATT 1947. The GATT was implemented as a preliminary agreement when it became apparent that the ratification of the Havana Charter of 1947 would meet resistance in the US Congress. This charter would have created the International Trade Organization (ITO) which would have constituted the third 'pillar' of the Bretton Woods system apart from the IMF and World Bank. The GATT and its Art. XX reflect the preferences of the 1940s. Article XX, for example, reflects the concerns of the 1940s by allowing for exemptions under the agreement if there is a shortage in certain goods.

93   See also Petersmann (1995, pp. 22–24). The only environmental case which partly found the approval of a GATT panel was the 1994 report on US taxes on automobiles. The luxury tax and the 'gas guzzler tax' were found not to treat imported cars less favourably than domestic automobiles, while the Corporate Automobile Fuel Economy Standards (CAFE) were found in violation with the US obligations under the GATT. However, the question

was concerning discrimination among domestic and foreign producers. Art. XX was not involved. In the press it was speculated that this decision deviated a bit from the 'hard line' of the earlier rulings because, just after the panel report in the US Congress, the ratification process of the WTO Agreements was on the agenda. For the panel report see General Agreement on Tariffs and Trade (1994b).

94 See General Agreement on Tariffs and Trade (1982).
95 See General Agreement on Tariffs and Trade (1987).
96 See General Agreement on Tariffs and Trade (1988).
97 See General Agreement on Tariffs and Trade (1991) and General Agreement on Tariffs and Trade (1994a).
98 See World Trade Organization (1996) and World Trade Organization (1997b).
99 See General Agreement on Tariffs and Trade (1991).
100 See General Agreement on Tariffs and Trade (1990).
101 However, the panel did not generally deny a country's right to forbid the consumption of certain substances, e.g. cigarettes.
102 See World Trade Organization (1997a). The panel report was adopted by the Dispute Settlement Body (DSB) on 13 February 1998.
103 See General Agreement on Tariffs and Trade (1990).
104 See General Agreement on Tariffs and Trade (1994b).
105 See, for example, *Economist* (1995, p. 67).
106 Hillman and Ursprung (1992, p. 198).
107 In the sociological literature, Petulla (1980) traces environmentalism, which focuses on the US, back to three basic perspectives on nature. Thereby he explains the desire of a lot of Greens to change the societies' value system. For an analysis of the roots of the German environmental movements, see, for example, Linse (1986).
108 See Chapter 4.
109 For a survey on the choice of taxes or standards in environmental policy from a public choice perspective, see Körber (1995).
110 Ursprung (1992, p. 19).
111 For a detailed theoretical analysis see Hillman and Ursprung (1992).

3. The Political Process: Lobbying Functions

3.1 INTRODUCTION

The preceding chapter introduced the rent-seeking approach in order to analyse ecological protectionism. Seeking politically contestable rents falls within the broader category of contests[1]. Other examples of contests are: wars, election campaigns and R&D races. Different aspects of such contests have been analysed in the literature. Much attention has been paid to the social costs of rent-seeking contests.[2] Dixit (1987), for example, analyses how the possibility of pre-commiting on the rent of one contestant influences effort levels. Reasons for under- or overdissipation are given by Tullock (1980), Hillman and Samet (1987), Hillman and Riley (1989) and Ursprung (1990). Dasgupta and Stiglitz (1988), Dasgupta (1986) and Leininger (1991) concentrate on R&D rivalry and patent competition.

Using the terminology of a military combat, 'one-sided submission' – as Hirshleifer (1989) noted – is a possible outcome of a contest. But under which circumstances will a player in a contest fight and when will he submit? When will an interest group spend lobbying contributions in order to raise environmental standards which raise a foreign or domestic rival's costs? Which strategy will the potentially disadvantaged group choose? Will this group enter the lobbying contest as well or will it refrain from lobbying activities? In a rent-seeking framework, this is very much the question concerning the mechanism which transforms lobbying outlays into political outcomes. In rent-seeking models, the technical tool for this transformation is the contest–success function (CSF) or lobbying function. By analysing its properties, conditions for 'war' and 'one-sided submission' are derived for the case of a Cournot competition. It turns out that the conditions for 'war' are restrictive. The fairly general results are also illustrated with two popular contest–success functions.[3] The Hirshleifer function (differences) can only produce corner solutions which correspond to a situation of 'one-sided submission', whereas the Tullock function (ratios) leads to 'war'.

If the design of the contest–success function is under the control of the master of the game trying to follow his or her own interests, 'war' or 'one-sided submission' will be chosen. The contest–success function can be made endogenous if one thinks, for example, of a contest as a lobbying game and of the master of the game as a regulator or state.[4] This means that regulators can use the choice of the lobbying function as a strategic variable to achieve their own goals. It is shown that they have no incentive to choose sophisticated contest–success functions like those proposed by Tullock (1980) or Hirshleifer (1989). If regulators are assumed to be revenue maximising in the sense that they will try to extract the maximum possible amount of lobbying outlays out of interest groups, they will always choose 'one-sided submission'. They can achieve this outcome by simply making a 'take-it-or-leave-it' offer.

The chapter proceeds as follows. In the context of a Cournot duopoly, first the conditions for 'one-sided submission' and 'war' in lobbying contests are derived by paying special attention to both firms' reaction functions in the lobbying contest. The analysis of lobbying functions is concluded with an application of our results to the renowned contest–success functions of Tullock (1980) and Hirshleifer (1989). In a second step, the idea of a state using the contest–success function to maximise its revenues is introduced. The results of the chapter are summarised in section 3.3.

3.2 WHEN TO FIGHT IN AN ASYMMETRIC TWO-PLAYER CONTEST

3.2.1 Theoretical Considerations

The analysis focuses on the strategic interaction between two players in a two-stage decision problem. In order to give a straightforward economic interpretation we use the terminology of a Cournot duopoly. Both competitors or firms, U_H and U_F, respectively, can influence the regulation by making contributions L_H and L_F to the state.[5] Depending on these lobbying efforts, the state can burden U_F with a tax, t, while U_H will never be subject to such regulation. Afterwards, both competitors choose their (homogeneous) outputs x_H and x_F, which are produced with constant-returns-to-scale technologies. Using the terminology of Salop and Scheffman (1983), one could think of firm U_H as engaging in 'raising rivals' costs' by influencing the state to implement regulation which disadvantages its competitor.[6] Thus, the tax, t, could, for example, be interpreted as a pollution tax if one assumes that U_F uses a 'dirtier' technology than U_H.[7] We, therefore, arrive at both firms' costs given by

$$C_H = b\, x_H, \tag{3.1}$$

$$C_F = (b + t)\, x_F, \tag{3.2}$$

where b indicates constant average and marginal production costs. The price, P, is determined by the (linear) inverse demand function

$$P = a - X \text{ with } X = x_H + x_F. \tag{3.3}$$

Maximising profits, π, for a given tax, t, leads to

$$\pi_H = \frac{1}{9}(a - b + t)^2, \tag{3.4}$$

$$\pi_F = \frac{1}{9}(a - b - 2t)^2. \tag{3.5}$$

Hence, we have introduced an asymmetry[8] into the model by a redistribution of market shares from U_F to U_H through the implementation of a tax.[9] Furthermore, in our model of an endogenous rent, the profits of U_H are higher and those of U_F lower than in the standard duopoly result.

At the first stage of the decision problem, the state may either implement a high tax rate, t_h, or a low one, t_l, $t_h > t_l$. As the equations (3.4) and (3.5) indicate, U_H has an interest in implementing the high tax rate, while U_F will try to keep the tax rate as low as possible and acts as a rent defender.[10] Nevertheless, it cannot be ensured that both firms will always engage in lobbying. Therefore, the lobbying process has to be analysed.

Lobbying is assumed to influence the probability of implementing the high tax rate, t_h. This probability depends on the form of the contest–success function q.[11] Thinking of lobbying as 'technology', we assume decreasing marginal returns from lobbying.

$$q: [L_H, L_F] \rightarrow [0,1]$$

with

$$\frac{\partial q}{\partial L_H} \geq 0, \frac{\partial q}{\partial L_F} \leq 0, \frac{\partial^2 q}{\partial L_H^2} \leq 0, \frac{\partial^2 q}{\partial L_F^2} \geq 0, q(0,0) = 0. \tag{3.6}$$

Both firms are assumed to be risk neutral and, therefore, maximising their expected profits ($E[\pi_H]$, $E[\pi_F]$). 'War' is the outcome of both firms' optimisation problems as long as the first-order (FOC_i) and second-order conditions (SOC_i) are satisfied. To ensure that it is profitable for the firms to engage in lobbying, an incentive-compatibility constraint has to be met.[12] In this framework the term is used in the sense that the expected profits of firm U_H, given that both firms spend their equilibrium lobbying outlays (L^*_H and L^*_F, respectively), have to be higher than its expected profits without any lobbying. U_H's maximisation problem can be written as follows

$$\max_{L_H} E[\pi_H] = q(L_H, L_F)\pi_1(t_h) + (1 - q(L_H, L_F))\pi_H(t_1) - L_H, \quad (3.7)$$

leading to

$$(\text{FOC}_H) \quad \frac{\partial E[\pi_H]}{\partial L_H} = 0, \quad (3.8)$$

$$(\text{ICC}_H) \quad E[\pi_H(L^*_H, L^*_F)] - E[\pi_H(0, 0)] \geq 0, \quad (3.9)$$

$$(\text{SOC}_H) \quad \frac{\partial^2 E\left[\pi_H\left(L^*_H, L^*_F\right)\right]}{\partial L_H^2} \leq 0. \quad (3.10)$$

U_F maximises its expected profit respectively.[13] For simplicity, we assume that in the case of a low tax rate no tax is levied on U_F's output ($t_1 = 0$). The high tax; t_h, is set equal to ½ $(a - b)$, which is the value where U_F drops out of the market.[14] Thus, the rent-seeking contest results in a game at stage 2 where either both competitors can earn symmetric Cournot duopoly profits or U_H can get a monopoly rent while U_F is forced to leave the market before subtracting lobbying outlays.

Using the implicit function rule, we calculate the slope of the reaction functions[15] (RF_i, $i = H, F$) for both firms' first-order conditions

$$\left. \frac{\Delta L_H}{\Delta L_F} \right|_{RF_H} = \begin{cases} -\dfrac{q_{HF}}{q_{HH}} & \text{for } L_H > 0 \\[3mm] \max\left[0, \dfrac{q_{HF}}{q_{HH}}\right] & \text{for } L_H = 0 \end{cases} \quad (3.11)$$

$$\left. \frac{\Delta L_H}{\Delta L_F} \right|_{RF_F} = \begin{cases} -\dfrac{q_{FH}}{q_{FF}} & \text{for } L_F > 0 \\[3mm] \max\left[0, -\dfrac{q_{FH}}{q_{FF}}\right] & \text{for } L_F = 0 \end{cases} \quad (3.12)$$

The slopes of the reaction functions[16] are the ratios of the cross derivative and the direct second derivative of the lobbying function. Both second derivatives indicate a change in the marginal effectiveness of lobbying. While q_{ii} represents the change due to a variation in a firm's own lobbying efforts, q_{ij} stands for the change in the probability, q, when the competitor shifts his efforts. It is known from the properties of the contest–success function given in equation (3.6) that $q_{HH} < 0$ and $q_{FF} > 0$. Thus, the cross derivatives become decisive for the slope of the reaction functions. Young's theorem, which is concerned with the cross derivatives of continuously differentiable functions, can be applied in this context and states that both cross derivatives are equal. Therefore, if $q_{HF} > 0$, then U_H's reaction function will have a positive slope while U_F's reaction function will be falling and vice versa.

Result 1:

(1) *If the cross derivative is globally positive, 'one-sided submission' will be the only equilibrium of the game, where only U_H spends a positive amount on lobbying contributions, while the competitor invests no resources in lobbying. In other words if*

$$q_{HL} \geq 0 \; \forall \; [L_H, L_I],$$

then

$$\left[L_H^* \Big|_{L_F = 0}, L_F = 0 \right]$$

is the only equilibrium.

(2) *A negative cross derivative for some L_i, L_j is necessary for 'war'.*

The proof of result 1 is straightforward:

(a) If the cross derivatives are globally positive or zero, the slope of U_F's reaction function will be negative if the lobbying outlays are not restricted to non-negative values. Due to the fact that they have to be larger than or equal to zero, the slope of U_F's reaction function is zero. Thus, globally, U_F's reaction function lies on the L_F-axes. Both reaction functions intersect at

$$\left[L_H^* \Big|_{L_F = 0}, L_F = 0 \right].$$

(b) If q_{HF} is smaller than zero for some L_i, L_j, U_F's reaction function is increasing according to (3.12) for this value or interval. Thus, there is some range in the L_H–L_F – space where U_F's lobbying contributions are strictly positive. If U_F's reaction function intersects here and no incentive-compatibility constraint is binding, there is an equilibrium with both firms engaging in lobbying.

This result provides strong conditions for 'war' and 'one-sided submission' in lobbying contests with a rather general contest–success function. 'War' will only occur if the marginal effectiveness of U_H's lobbying is reduced by an increase in U_F's outlays. Figure 3.1 provides us with an example for 'war'.

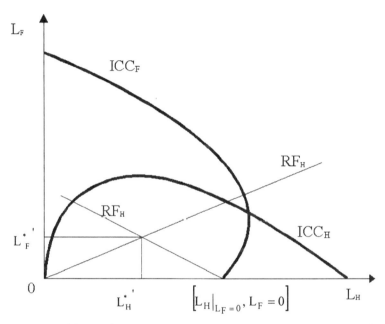

Figure 3.1 Lobbying functions – conditions for 'war' and 'one-sided submission'

'One-sided submission' will be the outcome if an increase in U_F's contributions improves the effectiveness of U_H's own efforts to influence the regulator. To interpret a positive cross derivative, one can think of situations where any kind of lobbying activity appreciates the public's sensitivity to the problem. At some airports, for example, competing airlines use different kinds of planes. Some firms own relatively quiet planes while others stick to older and noisier ones. It can be profitable for the firms with the newer and quieter planes to engage in lobbying for stricter noise reduction standards around airports, because noise is a highly sensitive topic in many urban areas.

If those airlines with noisier planes start 'counter-lobbying', the public's interest in this topic will be enhanced. Thus, lobbying could potentially worsen the situation of firms that are potentially subject to regulation.[17]

Thus, two qualitative prerequisites of 'war' in lobbying contests are derived.

(1) If U_F increases its lobbying outlays, the marginal effectiveness of U_H's lobbying has to be reduced. This may be a reasonable assumption for many contests, but the example above shows that this need not be the case.

(2) Only complicated lobbying processes in the sense of taking into account changes in the marginal effectiveness of one player's lobbying induced by a change in its competitor's outlays can result in 'war'. *A priori* it seems hard to believe that firms can observe or a regulator is able to signal such sophisticated properties of the lobbying process, or – in our terminology – the form of the function, q. Especially in the case of corruption it is likely that the regulator is restricted in signalling in detail how certain regulation can be bought.

Thus, strategic interaction in lobbying contests, for example, by the use of the Tullock function (see section 3.2.2), requires solid empirical justification for the two crucial qualitative properties described above. Skaperdas (1996) addresses this problem and axiomatises contest–success functions. An 'independence of irrelevant alternatives' axiom is mainly responsible for generating the class of additive functional forms, among them the ratio and the difference function. However, Skaperdas (1996) concludes that '[a]lthough helpful, axiomatizations by themselves are unlikely to settle the issue of appropriateness of a CSF for any particular contest situation'.

3.2.2 Illustration

Two lobbying functions are widely used in interest group models: the ratio model introduced by Tullock (1980) and the difference contest–success function by Hirshleifer (1989).[18] It is, therefore, analysed whether these functions lead us to 'war' or 'one-sided submission'.

Tullock assumes the probability of success to be the ratio of both players' lobbying contributions

$$q\ (L_H, L_F) = \frac{L_H}{L_H + L_F} \Leftrightarrow q\ (L_H, L_F) = \left(1 + \frac{L_F}{L_H}\right)^{-1}. \qquad (3.6')$$

Applying this function to our model and simultaneously solving both players' optimisation problems yields to the optimal lobbying outlays

$$L_H^* = \frac{4}{81} \frac{t\left(a-b-t\right)\left(2a-2b+t\right)^2}{\left(2a-2b-t\right)^2}, \tag{3.13}$$

$$L_F^* = \frac{16}{81} \frac{t\left(2a-2b+t\right)\left(a-b-t\right)^2}{\left(2a-2b-t\right)^2}. \tag{3.14}$$

They are strictly positive as long as the size of the market is large enough compared to the effective per-unit production costs ($a - b - t > 0$).

While no incentive-compatibility constraint is binding[19] and the second-order conditions are met, L_H^* and L_F^* denote the equilibrium lobbying contributions. The Tullock function, therefore, views 'war' as an outcome of a lobbying game. Thus, we obtain

Result 2:
For the Tullock function, 'war' exists as an interior Nash equilibrium while no incentive-compatibility constraint is binding.

Figure 3.2 provides a graphic interpretation, assuming $a = 100$, $b = 5$, and a prohibitive tax of 47.5 units.

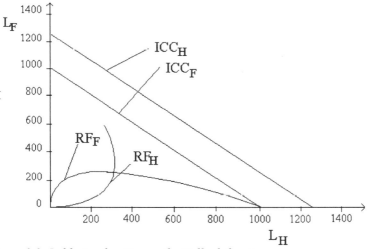

Figure 3.2 Lobbying functions – the Tullock function

Hirshleifer (1989) puts forward a logistic contest–success function which makes use of the difference between the players' lobbying outlays. For many problems, e.g. military combats, this function seems to be advantageous compared to Tullock's formulation. If one player refrains from making an effort the probability of success for its competitor does not automatically equal 1. Additionally it is, contrary to the Tullock contest–success function, defined at (0, 0) and takes the following form:

$$q\ (L_H, L_F) = \frac{1}{1 + \exp\{k(L_F - L_H)\}} \ . \qquad (3.6'')$$

While analysing whether Hirshleifer's logistic function will result in 'war' or 'one-sided submission' one discovers that 'war' is not a possible outcome under this contest–success function. For such an interior solution, maximisation would require both second-order conditions to be negative or zero. Because the second derivatives of the lobbying function, q, are identical, this requirement cannot be fulfilled simultaneously.[20] Thus, evaluated at the same point, it is impossible to meet these requirements at the same time. Hence, the reaction function is a best answer for only one player. Even the point $L_H = L_F$ does not constitute a maximum but rather a point of inflection.[21] This leads us to

Result 3:
The Hirshleifer contest–success function will never cause 'war' as an outcome of the contest.

The logistic lobbying function, therefore, belongs to a different class of functions than those described above, since it does not fulfil the basic requirement of being simultaneously concave in L_H and convex in L_F and cannot, therefore, generate interior equilibria.

3.3 THE DESIGN OF THE CONTEST

In the last section, the properties of 'war' and 'one-sided submission' were derived under the assumption that the regulator is just a passive broker of the pressure groups' different interests. Now one more step is introduced by analysing the conditions for both equilibria, taking into account that the regulator can use the choice of the contest–success function as a strategic variable to achieve its own goals. Which form of a contest will be chosen if the state switches from its passive role into the driving seat of our political vehicle?

Throughout this analysis a broad definition of lobbying outlays was employed. One might consider these outlays always as the efforts necessary to supply special information to the regulator or as the firms' donations to parties to support their political goals. Even presents to individual politicians or bureaucrats for their personal use are within our definition. Although the last alternative would probably cross the border to corruption in most countries, it is in any case advantageous for the regulator to maximise the sum of such lobbying contributions.

By implementing the high tax rate, t_h, the regulator can award a monopoly rent to U_H while the competitor is forced to leave the market. U_H's willingness to pay for this additional profit amounts to the expected value of the difference between the monopoly profit and the duopoly profit which it will earn in any case. Thus, U_H will invest at most $\pi^M - \pi^D - \varepsilon$, $\varepsilon \to 0$ in the lobbying contest if the probability of winning the contest is equal to one.[22] With $\varepsilon > 0$ the firm is strictly better off reaching the monopoly position. If the joint output of both competitors is bigger than in the monopoly case, total profits will be smaller.[23] Therefore, any outcome with both firms remaining in the market creates total profits, and thus total maximum lobbying contributions smaller than $\pi^M - \pi^D - \varepsilon$.

Result 4:

The maximum the regulator can appropriate from U_H in exchange for the granted rent is $\pi^M - \pi^D - \varepsilon$, $\varepsilon \to 0$.

By the monotonicity of the joint profits the regulator will always have to implement the high tax to maximise total profits. This leads us directly to

Result 5:

Every revenue-maximising political process will lead to 'one-sided submission' with only U_H engaging in lobbying if a contest–success function exists which generates 'one-sided submission' as an equilibrium.

In section 3.2 it was shown that in the case of an exogenous contest–success function two conditions have to be met in order for 'war' to be a possible outcome of the game. Although 'war' was possible, there were constraints on the existence of such an equilibrium. In the framework of a 'revenue-maximising regulator', 'one-sided submission' is the only equilibrium while a struggle with both firms engaging in lobbying is no longer possible.

Consequently, even if the state could overcome the informational constraints in signalling how to influence regulation, it would not be rational for it to use sophisticated contest–success functions. Such 'complicated' functions would only be necessary to generate 'war' as an equilibrium of the lobbying game, while the revenue-maximising outcome, however, can only be reached with 'one-sided submission'. This result can be achieved with a simple 'take-it-or-leave-it' mechanism.[24]

Lemma:
A revenue-maximising lobbying mechanism is given by

$$q(L_H, L_F) = \begin{cases} 1, & L_H = \pi^M - \pi^D - \varepsilon, \ L_F \in [0,\infty) \\ 0, & L_F \neq \pi^M - \pi^D - \varepsilon, \ L_F \in [0,\infty) \end{cases} \quad \text{and } t = \frac{1}{2}(a-b).$$

If U_H accepts the regulator's offer, it will be able to increase its profits by ε, while U_F will always suffer a loss.[25] Hence, $(L_H, 0)$ is the only equilibrium.

Thus, in our setting there is no room for real strategic interaction between firms because the state would not maximise its revenues if it implemented a contest–success function leading to 'war' as an equilibrium.

3.4 CONCLUSIONS

In this chapter the conditions for 'war' and 'one-sided submission' as an outcome of lobbying contests for the case of Cournot competition were analysed. As long as the lobbying function is exogenously given, both types of equilibria are possible.

Nevertheless, it was shown that 'war' as an equilibrium of the game has to meet two prerequisites. The marginal effectiveness of one player has to be decreased by an increase in its competitor's outlays. Thus, only sophisticated lobbying functions in the sense of having these cross effects are able to generate 'war'. Consequently, lobbying models with both players making outlays are restrictive. Applying our findings to the renowned Tullock and Hirshleifer functions we found that, while the first can generate 'war' as a possible equilibrium, the latter always leads to 'one-sided submission' due to its functional properties.

If one allows for a contest–success function endogenously chosen by a state maximising lobbying outlays, 'one-sided submission' is the only possible outcome. In such a framework 'war' is only possible if either the firms do not act as profit maximisers or the regulator does not behave rationally.

NOTES

1   This chapter is based on Körber and Kolmar (1996).
2   For a detailed survey of the literature see Nitzan (1994).
3   The terms 'contest–success function' and 'lobbying function' are used synonymously.
4   Throughout our analysis we use the terms 'regulator' and 'state' as synonyms.
5   To give an example for lobbying contributions, one can think of campaign contributions for political parties, perquisites for bureaucrats and politicians, etc.

6 Oster (1982) stresses the importance of regulation as a strategy to weaken competitors in the market place.

7 See Maloney and McCormick (1982).

8 The term 'asymmetry' is somewhat ambiguous in the literature. Dixit (1987), for example, uses the term to describe a different treatment of both competitors by the contest–success function.

9 In a general lobbying model, this is equivalent to a rent transfer from U_F to U_H.

10 Appelbaum and Katz (1986) formalised the idea of spending lobbying outlays in order to defend an existing rent, instead of making contributions in order to seek a politically contestable rent.

11 $(1 - q)$ denotes the probability of enacting the low tax rate.

12 The term is due to the literature on mechanism design.

13 Note that U_F's incentive compatibility constraint takes the following form: $E[\pi_F (L^*_H, L^*_F)] - E[\pi_F (L^*_H, 0)] \geq 0$. The difference in the firms' incentive compatibility constraints is due to the asymmetry built into the model. The 'prize' of the contest is a redistribution of market shares from U_F to U_H. Consequently, U_F will only use lobbying if U_H sets $L_H = 1$ because, otherwise, there is no such redistribution of market shares and U_F has no incentive to enter the contest. To meet U_F's incentive compatibility constraint, its expected profit with both firms spending lobbying outlays has to be larger than its expected profit with spending no lobbying contributions on rent defending despite U_H setting $L_H = 1$.

14 $\pi^0_F = (1/9) (a - b - 2t)^2 = 0 \Leftrightarrow t = (a - b)/2$.

15 They are called reaction functions despite the fact that they are only best answers as long as the relevant incentive compatibility constraint is not binding. Note that

$$q_{HF} = \frac{\partial^2 q}{\partial L_H \partial L_F}, \quad q_{FH} = \frac{\partial^2 q}{\partial L_F \partial L_H}, \quad q_{HH} = \frac{\partial^2 q}{\partial L_H^2}, \quad q_{FF} = \frac{\partial^2 q}{\partial L_F^2}.$$

16 In standard game theory this expression is used to calculate the local stability condition (see Fudenberg and Tirole (1993, p. 24). It is also employed by Dixit (1987) and Baik and Shogren (1992) to analyse the structural stability of simultaneous move games.

17 Gialloretto (1989) describes such lobbying activities at the Frankfurt/Main airport. In *Tagesanzeiger* (1997, p. 5) similar events were reported for the airport of Zürich-Kloten.

18 As throughout the whole analysis, we restrict our attention to the case of $N = 2$ players. Additionally, we assume the exponents to be one.

19 $ICC_H (L^*_H, L^*_F) = (1/81)[t (2a - 2b + t)^3 / (2a - 2b - t)^2] > 0,$
    $ICC_F (L^*_H, L^*_F) = (64/81) [t (a - b - t)^3 / (2a - 2b - t)^2] > 0.$

20 Both second-order conditions are described by

$$\frac{\partial^2 q}{\partial L^*_H} = \frac{k^2\left(-\exp\left\{2k\left(L_F - L_H\right)\right\} + \exp\left\{k\left(L_F - L_H\right)\right\}\right)}{\left(1 + \exp\left\{k\left(L_F - L_H\right)\right\}\right)^3} = \frac{\partial^2 q}{\partial L_F^2}.$$

21 $L_H = L_F$ is a point of inflection and not a saddle point because here the first derivatives of the players' maximisation problems are positive, the second derivatives equal zero, and the third are unambiguously negative.

22 π^M denotes the monopoly profit while π^D stands for the duopoly profit without any tax. ε is a very small amount of money.

23 The expansion in total output can, for example, be calculated according to U_H's output reaction function:

$$\frac{\partial x_H}{\partial x_F} = -\frac{1}{2} x_F.$$

Formally this means:

$$\left\{ \begin{array}{ll} \dfrac{\partial\left(\pi_H+\pi_F\right)}{\partial x_i}=0 & \text{for } x_H+x_F=X_M \\[2ex] \dfrac{\partial\left(\pi_H+\pi_F\right)}{\partial x_i}<0 & \text{for } x_H+x_F>X_M \end{array} \right\}.$$

24   It should be noted that, contrary to the assumption in (3.6), this mechanism is not twice continuously differentiable.

25   This means:

$$\pi_H\left(L_H, L_F\right) = \pi^D + \varepsilon > \pi_H\left(\overline{L_H}, L_F\right) = \pi^D, \ \overline{L_H} \neq L_H \text{ for } U_H, \text{ and}$$

$$\pi_F\left(L_H, 0\right) = 0 > \pi_F\left(L_H, L_F\right) \text{ for } U_F.$$

4. Raising Rivals' Costs with Environmental Policy: A Lobbying Approach

4.1 INTRODUCTION

This chapter uses the framework of 'raising rivals' costs' known from the preceding analysis. While, however, the focus thus far was on the properties of the lobbying function, here it is on the application of 'raising rivals' costs' to the process of environmental decision making. The model is extended by incorporating the special features of environmental legislation which will be discussed in the following paragraph. This new focus technically requires the extension of the static model by a second period and – in section 4.3 – the introduction of the environmentalists as an additional interest group. In order to keep the model tractable, the lobbying process is kept simpler than in the analysis of Chapter 3. For this purpose, a standard lobbying function is used.

Three features of environmental regulation make it – as pointed out earlier – particularly useful for protectionist interest groups. First, environmental regulation is legal under the WTO regime as long as its application is non-discriminatory. The definition of 'like products' in the auto panel decision[1] made clear that there is enough room for effectively discriminatory standards to be considered 'non-discriminatory' by the WTO. Second, once implemented, stricter environmental regulation is to a certain degree 'irreversible' in the political process. With strong environmentalist groups and a high public interest in environmental issues, one rarely observes that these standards are weakened again. Rapid advances in pollution abatement technologies, which made these abatement processes less costly, have regularly undermined industry's demands to decrease the level of environmental regulation again. Third, influential environmentalist pressure groups exist which can form potentially powerful coalitions with domestic interest groups.

It should be noted that, by its very nature, the concept of 'raising rivals' costs' can be interpreted in two ways. It can be a protectionist measure *vis-à-vis* foreign industries or a corporate strategy of an industry sub-group in an intra-industrial competition among subgroups of a domestic industry.

Within this study the first interpretation is used. For example, Swissair recently began advocating higher landing fees for noise-polluting planes at the airport of Zürich Kloten. Additionally, for certain types of planes, the regulation supported by Swissair will result in considerable restrictions regarding the times at which they are permitted to use the airport.[2] From the point of view of the world trading system, this is non-discriminatory regulation because it aims at certain types of planes and does not distinguish between domestic and foreign airlines. Swissair, however, can bear the costs of higher landing fees more easily than many of its foreign competitors because it has already replaced the majority of its noisier planes. A lot of foreign airlines will be burdened by this regulation more severely than the Swiss airline.[3] Another example for raising rivals' costs via advocating tighter environmental regulation was Chrysler's support for higher fuel-economy standards in the US at the beginning of the 1990s. At that time Chrysler was producing more small cars, which could more easily meet the standards than its foreign and domestic competitors.[4] It should be noted that the mere fact that protectionist interest groups use environmental regulation for purposes of raising rivals' costs does by no means imply that the measures are useless for protecting the environment. However, it is assumed throughout this study that the industry's interest in environmental regulation is predominantly protectionist.

This chapter analyses the three features of environmental regulation mentioned above. Section 4.2 focuses on the aspect of irreversibility. A lobbying contest between a domestic and a foreign firm is considered, one in favour of tighter regulation, one opposing it. If the tightening of the environmental standard fails, there will be the opportunity for a new contest, while once implemented the decision is final.[5] Section 4.3 explicitly incorporates the environmentalists as a third interest group into the game. Their influence on the introduction of a potentially discriminatory environmental tax is analysed.

4.2 FINAL DECISIONS IN ENVIRONMENTAL DECISION MAKING

4.2.1 Introduction

Lobbying for stricter environmental standards contains – as do many rent-seeking contests – a dynamic asymmetry. If one player succeeds, the game will end; if he loses, there will be another contest. Examples mentioned by Stephan and Ursprung (1998, p. 370) are the liberalisation of world trade in multilateral agreements and imperialistic wars. In the first case, the decision might be final in the sense that international competition can destroy the protectionist interest, while free traders can always try again to press for liberalisation. In an imperialistic war, a small country might reject the bids of the aggressor several times, with the possibility of final defeat.

In environmental decision making, the disadvantaged interest groups want to reverse the policy. This desire is – as already mentioned – usually undermined by advances in pollution abatement technology which becomes less costly over time. This considerably weakens the position of the protagonists of lower environmental standards.

Most conflicts can be interpreted in two ways: 'Conflict and settlement are usually interpreted as *dichotomous*. Rival nations are said to be at war or peace; a trade union may call a strike or else sign a collective bargaining contract; a lawsuit may be settled or else litigated in court.'[6] For environmental regulation, this view of contests implies the exclusion of foreign or domestic competitors from the domestic market, for example, by prohibiting a certain technology. In the case of pollution and noise reduction standards at airports, domestic firms can lobby for a complete ban on noisy planes. As long as the firms which are targeted by stricter environmental regulation cannot change their technology, they are excluded from the market. In this setting, firms might pursue lobbying strategies in which they either spend the maximum lobbying contributions or nothing. To employ a military terminology, they are either at 'war' or at 'peace'. This case will be referred to as the 'dichotomous' case. This 'all-or-nothing' setting describes an extreme form of 'raising rivals' costs'. The costs of one competitor are made prohibitive by the environmental regulation.

One can also think of less 'dramatic' scenarios in which the 'target' firm is burdened with costs which are far from being prohibitive. Accordingly, the firms' lobbying contributions are less likely to be fixed at the maximum amount or nothing. Additionally, Hirshleifer (1995, p. 168) points out that 'very often what looks like a dichotomous decision on a small time-scale becomes a *continuous* choice taking a longer perspective.'[7] To provide an example from environmental law for such a continuous choice, one can think of a standard which is not – compared to the dichotomous case – prohibitive but varies between zero and a market-excluding value. Throughout this section, such a setting will be referred to as the 'continuous' case.

Both interpretations of conflicts are possible and – as the examples show – important in the context of 'raising rivals' costs' with environmental policy. Thus, in section 4.2.2 a 'dichotomous' model is introduced in which a foreign rival can be burdened with a prohibitive costs.[8] Section 4.2.3 depicts the alternative interpretation, the 'continuous' case. To analyse the implications of the 'finality' of the environmental decision, the model is extended over two periods.

4.2.2 The Dichotomous Model

The static case
The framework We consider a two-player contest with a domestic and a foreign firm, denoted as U_H and U_F, respectively. They are assumed to be identical except for their technology. U_F is subject to potential governmental regulation. To stick to the example of airport regulation, the landing of noisy planes can be completely forbidden. Hence, once the regulatory measures are enacted, U_F has to drop out of the market and, consequently, its profits in the domestic market are reduced to zero. In this case, U_H earns the monopoly profit, π^M. If no action is taken at all, both firms will earn normal duopoly profits, π^D.[9]

The firms are assumed to be risk-neutral and to maximise their expected profits. They can influence the regulatory process by making lobbying contributions to the regulator. In this 'war-or-peace' setting, both competitors can either spend $L_i = 0$ or $L_i = 1$ with i = H, F. If both firms set their lobbying contributions equal to 1, the regulation will be implemented with a probability p_1.[10] If only U_H enters the lobbying-process, the implementation probability is equal to p_2. It is assumed that p_1 is always smaller than p_2.[11] This captures the idea that it is rational for U_F to engage in rent-avoiding lobbying in order to reduce the probability of being excluded from the market. If there is no lobbying at all, no regulation will be implemented with certainty. In other words, the probability of implementation is zero.

Both firms' decision-making process can be described by the game tree in figure 4.1.

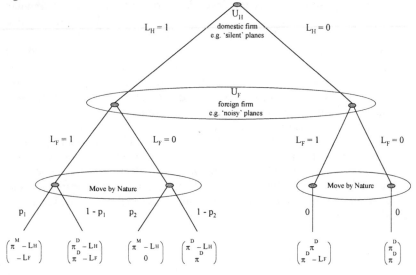

Figure 4.1 The dichotomous model – game tree in the static case

The game can be interpreted in the following way. U_H decides whether to engage in lobbying and sets $L_H = 1$ or $L_H = 0$. Simultaneously, U_F has to decide on its own lobbying outlays without knowing whether it is on the left or the right branch of the game tree. The probabilities depending on both firms' decisions can be found in table 4.1. Then, the regulation will be implemented with the probability p_1 if both firms invest in lobbying and with the probability p_2 if only U_H stays in the lobbying process. The difference in the size of the probabilities $(p_2 - p_1 > 0)$ indicates that, without U_F's 'counter-lobbying', U_H's chances to succeed in the political process are higher.

Table 4.1 The probabilities of the implementation of stricter environmental standards in the 'dichotomous' case

	$L_F = 0$	$L_F = 1$
$L_H = 0$	0	0
$L_H = 1$	p_2	p_1

Each firm will engage in lobbying if its expected profit with lobbying is higher than without it. The payoffs depicted in figure 4.1 reflect that if U_H wins the contest, it will earn a monopoly profit, π^M while U_F will be forced to leave the market. If no regulation is implemented, both firms will receive their duopoly profits, π^D.

Results First, the conditions are determined which have to be met in order to make it profitable for a firm to enter the lobbying contest. A firm will engage in lobbying if its expected profits with lobbying are higher than without.

$$L_H = \left.\begin{Bmatrix}1\\0\end{Bmatrix}\right|_{L_F=1} \Leftrightarrow \underbrace{p_1\pi^M + (1-p_1)\pi^D - L_H}_{\text{lobbying}} \begin{Bmatrix}\geq\\<\end{Bmatrix} \underbrace{\pi^D}_{\text{no lobbying}} \quad \text{if } L_H = 1.$$

Consequently, each firm's expected profits for both situations are calculated. This procedure gives us two sets of 'best responses' for each firm, one under the assumption that the competitor also spends lobbying contributions, one for the opposite case.

The complete results (equation 4.1' to equation 4.4") can be found in the appendices.[12] For example, U_H's 'best responses' for the case that U_F spends lobbying outlays ($L_F = 1$) are given by the equations (4.3') and (4.3").

Simplifying the equation and setting $L_H = 1$ leads us to the 'best responses':

$$L_H = \left\{ \begin{matrix} 1 \\ 0 \end{matrix} \right\|_{L_F = 1} \quad \Leftrightarrow \quad \underbrace{p_1\left(\pi^M - \pi^D\right)}_{\text{Gains from lobbying}} \left\{ \begin{matrix} \geq \\ < \end{matrix} \right\} \quad \underbrace{1}_{\text{Costs from lobbying}} . \qquad \begin{matrix} (4.3') \\ (4.3'') \end{matrix}$$

After having derived the four 'best responses', we must test which pairs of strategies are consistent with each other in order to obtain the pure strategy equilibria of the game. A 'two-sided lobbying contest', for example, is only a possible outcome if (4.3') and (4.1') can be fulfilled simultaneously

$$L_H = 1 \Leftrightarrow (\pi^M - \pi^D)\, p_1 \geq 1, \qquad (4.3')$$

$$L_F = 1 \Leftrightarrow \pi^D\, (p_2 - p_1) \geq 1. \qquad (4.1')$$

Both firms' strategies, (4.1') and (4.3'), will be consistent with each other if $p_2 > p_1$. According to (4.3'), U_H will engage in lobbying if its expected profit exceeds its expected costs. The expected profit is the difference between the monopoly profit and the duopoly profit, weighted with the probability of winning a two-sided lobbying contest (p_1). The expected costs are equal to the outlays which are normalised to one. U_F – according to (4.1') – will also stay in the contest if its expected gains, the duopoly profit weighted with ($p_2 - p_1$), exceeds its costs from lobbying.

By the same procedure,[13] three pure-strategy equilibria can be derived:

(1, 1)   (1, 0)   (0, 0).

Figure 4.2 depicts all equilibria in the p_1–p_2-space. The pure-strategy equilibria depend on four exogenous variables: π^M, π^D, p_1 and p_2. With $p_2 > p_1$, by definition there can be only pure strategy equilibria above the 45 degree-line in the p_2–p_1-space. While the absolute and relative size of the duopoly profit and the monopoly profit characterise features of the relevant market, the probabilities reflect the 'political environment'. They describe the regulator's responsiveness to lobbying for stricter environmental regulation. In a setting in which both probabilities are low, the policy maker will hardly be likely to implement tighter regulation if this is demanded in the political process. The reasons may be institutional constraints on the politicians' or bureaucrats' ability to appropriate lobbying contributions or a general un-willingness to use environmental regulation as a policy tool.

If both probabilities are high, the government is very likely to respond positively to the domestic firm's demand for stricter regulation. The foreign firm's influence in the political process is small because successful lobbying leads only to a very modest improvement for U_F. Although p_1 is by definition smaller than p_2, the probability p_2 remains high.

Alternatively, with a high p_2 compared to p_1, the government is only likely to follow the domestic firm's demand for stricter environmental policy as long as the foreign competitor does not enter the lobbying contest. As soon as the foreign industry starts to 'counter' lobby, the probability of implementation drops to a comparatively low p_1. Such an institutional setting reveals a high influence of the foreign firm on the domestic political process. One interpretation is that the foreigner potentially has the power to inflict harm on the domestic regulator, for example by asking its own government to challenge the particular regulation in the dispute settlement system of the WTO.

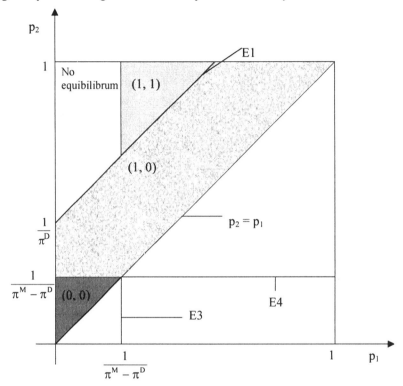

Constraints:

E1: $p_2 - p_1 - \dfrac{1}{\pi^D} = 0$ E3: $p_1 - \dfrac{1}{\pi^M - \pi^D} = 0$

E4: $p_2 - \dfrac{1}{\pi^M - \pi^D} = 0$

Figure 4.2 The dichotomous model – pure strategy equilibria in the static case

Hence, the institutional setting of the three pure-strategy equilibria depicted in figure 4.2 can be described as follows:

'Two-sided lobbying contest' (1, 1)   In this situation, both firms spend lobbying contributions in the environmental decision-making process. U_H presses for stricter environmental regulation in order to exclude U_F from the market, while U_F spends resources on 'rent-avoiding' in order to decrease the probability of being expelled from the market.

U_H enters the contest because p_2 and p_1 are beyond threshold values which are determined by its stake. This is equal to the difference between the monopoly and the duopoly profit (E4 and E3).[14] The higher U_H's expected profit from lobbying, the lower the probability of success the firm is willing to accept and still enter the contest. Consequently, with shrinking gains from lobbying, E3 will shift to the right, thereby reducing the area of a 'two-sided lobbying contest', while the area with no pure strategy equilibrium will expand.

The foreign firm's counter lobbying results in change of the probability of implementation from p_2 to p_1. In equilibrium, this difference has to be high enough to make it profitable for U_F to invest $L_F = 1$ in the contest (E1). In other words, if the foreign firm has only little political influence and its lobbying efforts only result in a small change from p_2 to p_1, it will not 'waste' its money on lobbying. The threshold probability which makes it worthwhile for the foreigner to enter the contest depends on π^D. The smaller the profit without stricter environmental regulation, the less likely foreign lobbying activities are. In other words, if the foreign firm has hardly any profits to defend, it will consequently make no efforts to counteract 'hostile' environmental regulation.

In the institutional framework that belongs to a 'two-sided lobbying contest', the government is likely to use environmental regulation. Protection of natural resources might be a very sensible topic and measures undertaken to reduce, for example, pollution will be widely appreciated. Beyond this model, one could think of a strong environmental movement which already laid the foundation for stricter environmental laws. As soon as the domestic industry joins the contest, it becomes very likely that the government reacts positively to such demands. Nevertheless, the foreign competitor has some access to the domestic political process because he is able to decrease the probability of implementing the 'offending' regulation by setting $L_F = 1$.

'One-sided lobbying contest' (1, 0)   In a 'one-sided lobbying contest', only U_H engages in lobbying in order to exclude its rival from the market. U_F does not invest in lobbying in order to influence the political process in its favour. In the language of a military conflict, one can speak of a 'one-sided submission' from U_F's point of view.

U_H enters the contest because p_2 exceeds a minimum value determined by its expected gain from lobbying (E4), which is equal to the difference between the monopoly and the duopoly profit. Thus, the larger U_H's potential gain from environmental regulation, the smaller the threshold value of p_2 for it to enter the contest.

The foreign firm cannot improve its situation by investing in lobbying. The probabilities, p_2 and p_1, are too 'similar'. Hence, the foreign firm is not able to gain enough in terms of a decrease in the probability that stricter regulation will be implemented.

With an increasing stake for U_F, the area of 'one-sided lobbying contest' decreases because the restriction (E1) in figure 4.2 moves closer to the 45-degrees line. U_H will always enter the lobbying contest as long as p_2 is larger than the threshold given by its expected gain from lobbying (E4). With an increasing $\pi^M - \pi^D$, the threshold value of p_2 will decrease and the region of pure-strategy equilibrium will grow at the expense of the 'no-lobbying area' $(0, 0)$.

'No-lobbying contest' $(0, 0)$ Again, U_F will not set $L_F = 1$ because p_2 and p_1 are too 'similar' and the potential reduction in the probability is, therefore, too small. U_F's situation is structurally the same as in the 'one-sided lobbying contest' $(1, 0)$.

The conditions are different for U_H. Both probabilities, p_2 and p_1, are too small to make it profitable for the domestic firm to engage in lobbying. U_H's lobbying strategy is determined by the difference between the monopoly and the duopoly profit (E3 and E4). In this equilibrium, the domestic firm cannot win enough by entering the contest.

The equilibrium $(0, 0)$ is likely when lobbying efforts can hardly influence the regulator in favour of implementing environmental regulation. This might apply to an institutional frame where the policy-maker either objects to state interventions in general or environmental legislation in particular.[15]

Thus far, the analysis developed a basic political economic model of raising rivals' costs with environmental policy. We showed that, depending on the variables forming the political and economic framework of the country, three equilibria exist in pure strategies. In military terms, there is peace, war, and one-sided submission between the domestic and the foreign firm.

The inter-temporal model
The framework   In this section, the existing framework is extended by a second period in order to address two important problems. First, the 'finality' of successful lobbying for stricter environmental regulation is introduced into the model. Second, within this framework, the conditions are analysed under which the domestic and the foreign firm change their strategies over time.

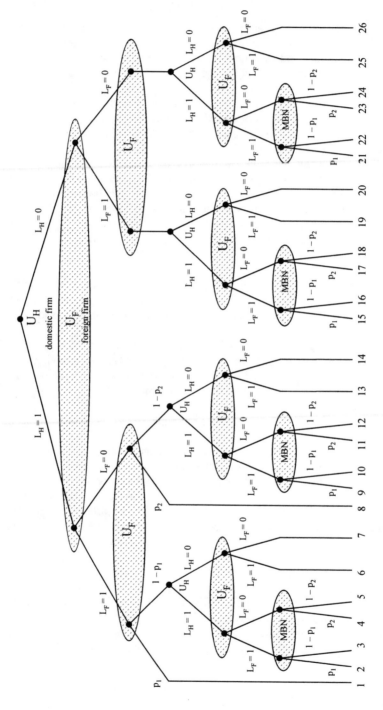

Figure 4.3 The dichotomous model – game tree in the inter-temporal case

Do equilibria in pure strategies exist in which one or both firms switch from lobbying to no lobbying or vice versa?

The static game is modified in the following way. If U_H was not successful with its lobbying attempts in the first period, there will be a second contest in the next period. If U_F lost in the first period and the stricter regulation was enacted, the new rules cannot be contested again. Thus, the political process concerning environmental law contains a strong feature of irreversibility. This game is depicted in figure 4.3 and the corresponding payoffs of period 1 can be found in the appendices while the payoffs of period 2 remain the same as those depicted in figure 4.1.

In the first period, U_H decides whether to set L_H equal to 1 or to zero. Again, U_F does not know what its competitor's decision in the lobbying contest was when it had to decide what to do. As in the static case, the probability of implementing the environmental regulation in a 'two-sided lobbying contest' is lower than in a one-sided contest ($p_2 > p_1$). It is also assumed that the exogenous probabilities are the same for both periods and that there is no time discount rate.[16]

With stricter regulation already implemented in the first period, the domestic firm will receive a monopoly profit in each period and has to spend lobbying contributions only once. Consequently, in the same situation, the foreign firm is excluded from the market for both periods and makes no profits at all.

If, however, no stricter rules are implemented in the first period, the domestic U_H will be able to lobby for the stricter standards in the second period again. In terms of profits, this means that both firms earn a duopoly profit in the first period. In the next period, the game starts again which might lead to the monopoly profit for U_H and zero profits for U_F, or to a duopoly profit for both.

Results The model is solved by backward induction. The pure strategy subgame equilibria in period 2 are the same as in the static case. Hence, we obtain a 'two-sided lobbying contest', a 'one-sided lobbying contest', and a 'no lobbying contest' in the second period. In period 1, for each of these subgame equilibria, the firms' 'best responses' have to be calculated.

$$L_{H1} = \left\{\begin{matrix}1\\0\end{matrix}\right\}\Bigg|_{L_{F1}=1} \Leftrightarrow p_1 \underbrace{\left(2\pi^M - L_{H1}\right)}_{\substack{\text{Stricter regulation in}\\\text{period 1}}} + \underbrace{(1-p_1)\left(2\pi^D + p_1\left(\pi^M - \pi^D\right) - 2L_{H1}\right)}_{\substack{\text{No stricter regulation in}\\\text{period 1}}}$$

$$\underbrace{}_{\text{Lobbying}}$$

$$\left\{\begin{matrix}\geq\\<\end{matrix}\right\}2\pi^D + p_1\left(\pi^M - \pi^D - L_{H1}\right).$$

Rearranging and setting $L_{H1} = 1$ leads us to

$$L_{H1} = \left\{ \begin{matrix} 1 \\ 0 \end{matrix} \right\} \bigg|_{L_{F1}=1} \Leftrightarrow \underbrace{\left(\pi^M - \pi^D\right)p_1(2 - p_1) + p_1}_{\text{Gains from lobbying}} \left\{ \begin{matrix} \geq \\ < \end{matrix} \right\} \underbrace{1}_{\substack{\text{Costs from} \\ \text{lobbying}}} . \quad \begin{matrix} (4.15') \\ (4.15'') \end{matrix}$$

The complete results (equations 4.5' to 4.16'') can be found in the appendices.[17] For example, we derive the reaction equations 4.15' and 4.15'' from U_H's maximisation problem. They belong to a setting with a 'two-sided lobbying contest' in period 2. Then U_H's lobbying strategy for the first period will be determined by[18]

By the same procedure, four sets of 'best responses' for each subgame equilibrium of period 2 are obtained in appendix 3. Again, it has to be tested whether the firms' strategies are consistent with each other. For a 'two-sided lobbying contest' in both periods, for example, it has to be tested whether 4.13' and 4.15' can be fulfilled simultaneously.[19]

$$L_{F1} = 1 \Leftrightarrow \pi^D (p_2 - p_1) (2 - p_1) - p_2 + p_1 \geq 1, \qquad (4.13')$$

$$L_{H1} = 1 \Leftrightarrow (\pi^M - \pi^D) p_1 (2 - p_1) + p_1 \geq 1. \qquad (4.15')$$

Both conditions can be fulfilled simultaneously. Hence, an equilibrium exists in which both firms engage in lobbying in both periods.

Using the same procedure, we obtain the following pure strategy equilibria for the inter-temporal game which are also depicted in figure 4.4.[20]

$$\begin{pmatrix} 0, & 0 \\ 0, & 0 \end{pmatrix}, \begin{pmatrix} 1, & 0 \\ 0, & 0 \end{pmatrix}, \begin{pmatrix} 1, & 0 \\ 1, & 0 \end{pmatrix}, \begin{pmatrix} 1, & 1 \\ 1, & 0 \end{pmatrix}, \begin{pmatrix} 1, & 1 \\ 1, & 1 \end{pmatrix}.$$

In the inter-temporal case, two kinds of pure strategy equilibria exist. Either at least one firm changes its strategy over time or U_H and U_F pursue the same equilibrium strategy in both periods. While the interpretation of the political and economic environment in the cases with the same strategy in both subgames is very much the same as those in the static case, the equilibria with changes in at least one firm's strategy needs more interpretation.[21]

'One-sided lobbying contest' in period 1 and 'no-lobbying contest' in period 2 The domestic firm will always engage in lobbying as long as the probability of winning a 'one-sided lobbying contest' is sufficiently high. This 'minimum p_2', which is determined by U_H's stake, is different in both periods. In the first period (E7), it is lower than in the second period (E4) because U_H's expected gains from lobbying are decreasing over time.

Lobbying in the first period gives the domestic firm the chance to get the monopoly profit twice. Entering the lobbying contest in the second period means that it has already had a duopoly profit in the first period and only has a chance to get the monopoly profit once but has to invest twice $L_{Hj} = 1$.[22]

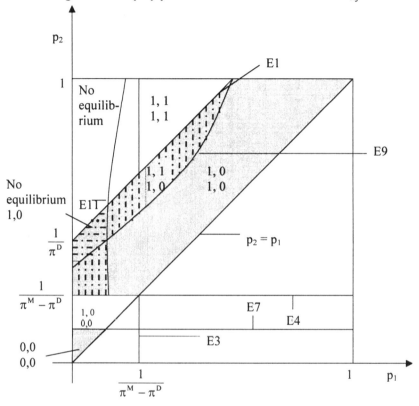

Constraints:

E1: $p_2 - p_1 - \dfrac{1}{\pi^D} = 0$

E3: $p_1 - \dfrac{1}{\pi^M - \pi^D} = 0$

E7: $p_2 - \dfrac{1}{2\left(\pi^M - \pi^D\right)} = 0$

E4: $p_2 - \dfrac{1}{\pi^M - \pi^D} = 0$

E9: $(p_2 - p_1)\,\pi^D\,(2 - p_2) - 1 = 0$

E11: $(\pi^M - \pi^D)\,p_1\,(2 - p_2) - 1 + p_2 = 0$

Figure 4.4   The dichotomous model – pure strategy equilibria in the inter-
            temporal case

The foreign firm stays out of the contest in both periods because it cannot benefit enough from lobbying. Setting $L_{Fj} = 1$ means investing resources in order to 'switch' from the higher p_1 to a lower p_2. In this equilibrium, p_1 and p_2 are too 'similar' and, hence, it is not rational for U_F to invest $L_{Fj} = 1$ in exchange for only a slight decrease in the probability of implementing stricter environmental regulation. The area of this equilibrium in the p_2–p_1-space will shrink if U_H's stake (E7 or E4) or U_F's stake (E1) will rise.

'Two-sided lobbying contest' in period 1 and 'one-sided lobbying contest' in period 2 In this equilibrium, the foreign firm changes its strategy over time. While it set $L_{F1} = 1$ in the first period, it stays out of lobbying in the second period. Again, the difference between the probability of winning a 'one-sided lobbying contest' and the probability of being successful in a 'two-sided lobbying contest' has to be large enough.

In comparison to a 'two-sided lobbying contest' in both periods, this time the foreign firm only has an incentive to participate in the lobbying process in the first period. This is due to the fact the U_F's expected loss from stricter environmental regulation is decreasing over time. The implementation of stricter environmental standards in period 1 causes U_F to loose the duopoly profit twice due to the 'irreversibility' of the regulation. Consequently, U_F is willing to accept a smaller difference between p_2 and p_1 in the first period than in the second period.

The interpretation concerning U_H's strategies does not change too much compared to the static model. As soon as p_2 is above a certain threshold (E7 in the first period, E4 in the second period), U_H starts to invest in lobbying. In addition, an area in figure 4.4 exists in which there is no pure strategy sub-game equilibrium in period 1, and a 'one-sided lobbying contest' in period 2.[23]

4.2.3 The Continuous Model

The framework
The model considered in the last section described a dichotomous setting where the competitors were either at 'war' or at 'peace' to stick to the terminology of Hirshleifer (1995). This scenario, which is frequently applied to models, is appropriate for analysing strategies of raising rivals' costs with environmental policy as long as the outcome is an 'all-or-nothing' solution, such as in the preceding game. Either the domestic firm earns a monopoly rent and its foreign rival is excluded from the domestic market, or no environmental regulation is enacted at all.

However, if, for example, the domestic country prescribes a tax on pollution instead of mandating a certain technology, usually no competitor is excluded from the market. Regularly, the industries have to pay according to the degree of the pollution. There is still room for raising rivals' costs by lobbying for stricter environmental standards, as long as the firms are treated differently by the regulation.[24] In this case, it is not reasonable to assume that the firms spend either the maximum amount on lobbying outlays or nothing. We will, therefore, use a contest–success function (CSF) – as discussed in chapter 3 – as a mechanism to determine the probability of winning the contest.

The continuous model to be introduced builds upon the framework of the dichotomous model. Again, a domestic and a foreign firm (U_H and U_F, respectively) compete in the domestic market. Environmental regulation takes the form of a discriminatory pollution fee per unit of output. For simplicity, we assume that, if implemented, stricter environmental regulation will not burden U_H, while U_F will have to pay a (fixed) environmental tax, t.[25] As in the dichotomous case, the game has a time horizon of two periods. In the first period, both firms simultaneously decide how much to spend in the lobbying process in order to determine whether the tax, t, is implemented or not. Afterwards they decide on their output. If the environmental taxation is introduced, the decision is 'final' in the sense that there will be no lobbying contest in the second period.[26] If there was no stricter regulation in the first period, there will be another contest in period 2.

The game is solved by backward induction. We use the same 'economic part' of the model as the one introduced by the equations 3.1 to 3.4 in chapter 3 with a linear inverse demand function, P, the same constant costs per unit, b, for both firms, and the environmental tax, t, per unit of U_F's output. Cournot competition in quantities leads again to the results known from chapter 3.[27]

$$\pi_H = \frac{1}{9}(a - b + t)^2,$$

(3.4)

$$\pi_F = \frac{1}{9}(a - b - 2t)^2.$$

(3.5)

The political process can be described by a standard contest–success function in which L_{Hj} and L_{Fj} denote the lobbying contributions of U_H and U_F in period j, respectively.[28] Therefore, the probability of implementing the environmental regulation in period j is[29]

$$q_j = \frac{L_{Hj}}{L_{Hj} + L_{Fj}} \quad \text{with } j = 1, 2.$$

(4.17)

For the second period, we define s_H as U_H's stake in the lobbying process. It is the difference between its profit with $t > 0$ and its profit with $t = 0$, π^D.[30]

U_F's stake, s_F, is the difference between its expected profit without any tax and its profits with a positive tax

$$s_H = \pi_H\big|_{t>0} - \pi_H\big|_{t=0}, \tag{4.18}$$

$$s_F = \pi_H\big|_{t=0} - \pi_H\big|_{t>0}. \tag{4.19}$$

Substituting 3.4 and 3.5 in 4.18 and 4.19 leads to

$$s_H = \frac{1}{9} t (2a - 2b + t), \tag{4.18'}$$

$$s_F = \frac{4}{9} t (a - b - t). \tag{4.19'}$$

For a sufficiently large market, a, U_F's stake is always larger than that of U_H. In other words, $s_F > s_H$ will be always valid.

Both firms are risk neutral and have perfect information. Both firms maximise their expected profits in the second period

$$E(\pi_{H2}) = q_2 \, \pi_{H2}\big|_{t>0} + (1 - q_2) \, \pi_{H2}\big|_{t=0} - L_{H2} \tag{4.20}$$

$$E(\pi_{F2}) = q_2 \, \pi_{F2}\big|_{t>0} + (1 - q_2) \, \pi_{F2}\big|_{t=0} - L_{F2} \tag{4.21}$$

Substituting in 4.18' and 4.19' leads to

$$E(\pi_{H2}) = \pi^D + q_2 \, s_H - L_{H2} \tag{4.20'}$$

$$E(\pi_{F2}) = \pi^D - q_2 \, s_F - L_{F2} \tag{4.21'}$$

Equations 4.20' and 4.21' indicate that, without any environmental tax ($t = 0$), both firms would have earned a duopoly profit. With a tax, however, U_H's profit is increased by s_H multiplied by q_2 while U_F's profit is decreased by s_F multiplied by q_2. Again, it should be noted that $s_F > s_H$ and, therefore, U_H wins less than U_F loses. The lobbying contributions spent by the firms engaged in the contest are L_{H2} and L_{F2}.

A Cournot–Nash concept is applied to the firms' contest. Differentiating 4.20' and 4.21' with respect to L_{H2} and L_{F2}, leads to the firms' reaction functions, which can be solved for L^*_{H2} and L^*_{F2} simultaneously. The firms' optimal lobbying contributions in period 2 are:

$$L^*_{H2} = \frac{s_H^2 s_F}{\left(s_H + s_F\right)^2} \tag{4.22}$$

$$L^*_{F2} = \frac{s_H s_F^2}{\left(s_H + s_F\right)^2} \tag{4.23}$$

These optimal lobbying contributions depend solely on both firms' stakes, s_H and s_F. Equations 4.22 and 4.23, are used in combination with the firms' objective functions, given by 4.20' and 4.21'. This leads us to the optimal profits of U_H and U_F in period 2 which are denoted π^*_{H2} and π^*_{F2}

$$\pi^*_{H2} = \pi^D + \frac{s_H^3}{\left(s_H + s_F\right)^2}, \tag{4.20''}$$

$$\pi^*_{F2} = \pi^D - \frac{s_H s_F \left(s_H + 2 s_F\right)}{\left(s_H + s_F\right)^2}. \tag{4.21''}$$

In period 1, both firms face a similar maximisation problem[31]

$$E\left(\pi_{H1}\right) = \pi^D + q_1 \left(\pi^D + 2 s_H\right) + \left(1 - q_1\right) \pi^*_{H2} - L_{H1}, \tag{4.24}$$

$$E\left(\pi_{F1}\right) = \pi^D + q_1 \left(\pi^D - 2 s_F\right) + \left(1 - q_1\right) \pi^*_{F2} - L_{F1}. \tag{4.25}$$

It follows from equation 4.24 that for the case in which environmental taxation is implemented in the first period, U_H will earn twice the duopoly profit plus twice s_H. This is due to the fact that if U_H succeeded in the first period, there will be no lobbying contest in the second period. If, however, there is no implementation of the tax in the first period, U_H will get the duopoly profit in $j = 1$ and has the chance to lobby again in the second period. The expected profit for such a lobbying contest in the second period is stated by equation 4.20''. According to 4.25, if the environmental tax is implemented in period 1, U_F will earn the duopoly profit in each period diminished by s_F in $j = 1, 2$. If, however, U_H's attempt to raise rival's costs fails in the first place, U_F can enjoy the duopoly profit in period 1 and might face a second contest.

Applying the Cournot–Nash concept to the contest leads to both firms' optimal lobbying contributions in period 1[32]

$$L_{HI}^{*} = \frac{s_H^{\,2}s_F\left(s_H^{\,2} + 4s_Hs_F + 2s_F^{\,2}\right)^2\left(s_H^{\,2} + 2s_Hs_F + 2s_F^{\,2}\right)}{\left(s_H + s_F\right)^2\left(4s_Hs_F^{\,2} + 5s_H^{\,2}s_F + s_H^{\,3} + 2s_F^{\,3}\right)^2}, \quad (4.26)$$

$$L_F^{*} = \frac{s_Hs_F^{\,2}\left(s_H^{\,2} + 4s_Hs_F + 2s_F^{\,2}\right)\left(s_H^{\,2} + 2s_Hs_F + 2s_F^{\,2}\right)^2}{\left(s_H + s_F\right)^2\left(4s_Hs_F^{\,2} + 5s_H^{\,2}s_F + s_H^{\,3} + 2s_F^{\,3}\right)^2}. \quad (4.27)$$

These terms can be re-written as

$$L_{HI}^{*} = \frac{s_H^{\,2}s_F\alpha^2\beta}{\gamma} \quad (4.26')$$

$$L_{FI}^{*} = \frac{s_Hs_F^{\,2}\alpha\beta^2}{\gamma} \quad (4.27')$$

with

$$\alpha = \left(s_H^{\,2} + 4s_Hs_F + 2s_F^{\,2}\right),$$

$$\beta = \left(s_H^{\,2} + 2s_Hs_F + 2s_F^{\,2}\right),$$

$$\gamma = \left(s_H + s_F\right)^2\left(4s_Hs_F^{\,2} + 5s_H^{\,2}s_F + s_H^{\,3} + 2s_F^{\,3}\right)^2.$$

Results The 'irreversibility' of the political process with respect to the introduction of stricter environmental standards has strong implications for the results of the model. As in the dichotomous model, U_H's expected gain from stricter environmental regulation decreases over time. The same holds true for U_F's expected loss from stricter standards. This forces both firms to adopt lobbying strategies in period 2, other than those used in period 1. In period 1, both firms lobbying contributions are higher than in period 2. Without a dynamic asymmetry, they would spend the same amount in both periods. In period 1, U_F generally spends more lobbying contributions than U_H. The reverse result may occur, but only for very high tax rates, t.[33]

In the second period, the foreign firm will always invest more than its domestic rival. This is due to the fact that U_F has 'more to lose' ($s_F > s_H$) than U_H can win. The firms' stakes determine their lobbying contribution.

4.3 THE GREENS' INFLUENCE ON ENVIRONMENTAL DECISION MAKING

4.3.1 Introduction

This section extends the analysis of raising rivals' costs with lobbying for stricter environmental regulation. It explicitly incorporates the environmentalists' influence on environmental decision making. A two-stage decision process is considered. First, it is decided whether to introduce environmental taxation, then the design of the tax is determined. In this political economic model, a foreign and a domestic firm, and environmentalists are the interest groups determining the policy outcome.

The literature on this issue is mainly concerned with two-player games. Either a domestic and a foreign firm compete against each other for trade policy goals or environmentalists and a homogenous industry influence the choice of environmental policy instruments.[34] There are only a few examples with two industries and an environmental interest group in the political process. Among these exceptions are Hillman and Ursprung (1992) and Hillman and Ursprung (1994a), who incorporate the environmentalists' influence in an 'interest-group-cum-electoral-competition model' known from trade policy making.

Within the framework of the continuous model presented in the last section, a first intuition suggests that additional lobbying on the part of the 'Greens' should increase the probability of implementing stricter environmental regulation. However, in standard models of lobbying, using a Nash equilibrium concept, Ursprung (1990) showed that 'if the politically allocated prize is a public good, the average stake of the individual rent-seekers represents an upper bound to total political outlays'.[35] In other words, in a lobbying game in which the contested prize has such characteristics, 'typical public good problems' with respect to the provision of the firms' lobbying outlays arise. Using these results, Hillman and Ursprung (1992) showed that a fixed amount of lobbying outlays spent by environmentalists who support the protectionist interest reduces the outlays of the other protectionists by exactly the same amount. Hence, the lobbying outlays of the 'pro-protectionist coalition' remain constant. It is, therefore, straightforward that the probability of implementing the desired regulation is not increased by the environmentalists' lobbying contributions.

This reasoning seems to leave little room for incorporating environmentalists in a model of 'raising rivals' costs'. However, this view neglects the two-stage nature of the environmental decision-making process. This analysis will show that the structure of the decision process enables the environmentalists to influence the probability of introducing stricter environmental regulation. The decision on an environmental tax usually consists of two parts:

- First, a general decision in favour or against the use of environmental taxation is taken.
- Second, the design of the tax is decided upon.

Such an interpretation corresponds to the distinction between high and low track measures of trade policy made by Finger *et al.* (1982). While high track measures are made in the public view, for example in Congress, low track measures are dealt with in committees or by government agencies. This distinction makes it clear that there are two consecutive lobbying processes involved. In the first stage, lobbying addresses a wide audience to determine whether environmental taxation will be introduced. At this stage, lobbying contributions are likely to be spent on media campaigns, etc. Later, lobbying outlays are used to influence some committee members or experts of political parties in favour or against a certain design of tax.

4.3.2 The Framework

Three interest groups are considered in this two-staged lobbying process: a domestic firm, U_H, a foreign firm, U_F, and environmentalists, E. In the first stage, it is decided whether or not to introduce an environmental tax. If the pollution tax[36] was generally approved, the focus of the second stage will be on the design of the tax. There are two possible tax patterns:

- a uniform tax rate, t, which burdens both firms with the same costs or
- a non-uniform tax rate with t_H and t_F as respective tax rates for U_H and U_F.[37]

The rationale for such discrimination between firms might be that their products have different environmental side effects. One could think of a regulation, for example, which treats cars with and without catalytic converters differently. The discussion of product-related environmental measures in section 2.4.3 already suggested that such classifications often result in a differential treatment of domestic and foreign producers.

The tax system has the following structure: In the non-uniform tax case, U_F's tax rate is at least twice as high as U_H's tax rate ($t_F > 2\,t_H$).[38] Furthermore, the uniform tax rate is lower than the unweighted average of the non-uniform tax rates, $t < \frac{1}{2}\,(t_H + t_F)$.

Hence, if a non-discriminatory tax rate is introduced, the foreign firm's additional costs will be higher than those of its domestic rival. Consequently, there is room for U_H to engage in lobbying in order to raise the foreign firm's costs. U_F, in turn, can engage in 'counter' lobbying. The environmentalists can spend a fixed amount of lobbying contributions, L_{gj} with j = 1, 2 on both stages of the political process.[39] After the political decisions have been made, both firms will determine their output quantities. The structure of the game is depicted in figure 4.5.

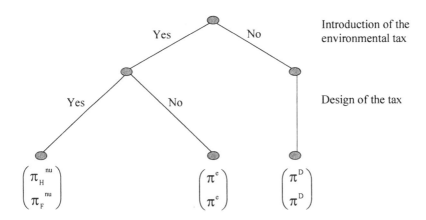

Figure 4.5 The introduction of an environmental tax – game tree

The 'economic' part of the model is already known from chapter 3 and the preceding section. The only exception is that U_H's tax rate is not set equal to zero. Consequently, Cournot output maximisation for a given non-uniform tax rate leads to the following profit functions for U_H and U_F, respectively[40]

$$\pi_H^{nu} = \frac{1}{9}(a - b - 2t_H + t_F)^2, \tag{4.28}$$

$$\pi_F^{nu} = \frac{1}{9}(a - b + t_H - 2t_F)^2. \tag{4.29}$$

The profits depend on the market size, a, constant per-unit production costs, b, and both firms' tax rates, t_H and t_F. With a uniform tax rate ($t = t_H = t_F > 0$), both firms earn the same profits, π^e, which are lower than in the case of no taxation. Hence, if the tax was designed as a uniform tax rate at stage 2, neither U_H nor U_F would have an incentive to lobby for the introduction of a tax rate at all during stage 1.

However, U_H's expected profits will be increased by a non-uniform tax rate while U_F's are decreased. The expectation that the tax is designed as a non-uniform tax rate in stage 2 can give U_H an incentive to lobby in favour of the introduction of an environmental tax in stage 1 in order to raise U_F's costs.

In the model, π^D represents the duopoly profit each firm can obtain in the case without any taxation ($t_1 = t_2 = 0$) while π_H^{nu} and π_F^{nu} (assuming $t_F > 2\,t_H$) are the profits of U_H and U_F under a regime of a non-uniform tax rates. The profit under a uniform tax rate ($t_H = t_F = t > 0$) is denoted by π^e.

The players' interests
The profits, which depend on the structure of the tax system, determine the interest groups' preferences with respect to a tax design.

The domestic firm U_H will gain by the introduction of a non-uniform environmental tax rate. This setting will be advantageous to a no-tax situation, which will be preferred to a uniform tax rate. Hence, U_H's preferences can be summarised by $\pi_H^{nu} > \pi^D > \pi^e$.

The foreign firm U_F is best off in a no-tax situation, which is preferable to a uniform tax rate. Firm F is worst off with a non-uniform tax rate. It follows: $\pi^D > \pi^e > \pi_F^{nu}$.

Environmentalists The environmentalists are considered to be interested in the reduction of the pollution creating activity. Since pollution increases with production, the Greens are assumed to aim at decreasing the firms' joint output. Due to the structure of the tax system, environmentalists prefer a non-uniform tax system to a uniform tax system because it leads to a larger output reduction. Both tax systems, however, are preferred to a situation of no taxation at all. Hence, the Greens will always engage in lobbying in favour of the introduction of environmental taxation in the first stage and will spend lobbying outlays in order to push for a non-uniform tax rate in stage 2.

The political process
As in the preceding section, a contest–success function of the type proposed by Tullock (1980) is at the core of the political process. It is the same for both stages of the decision process.[41] The probability of success in stage j is denoted by q_j with $j = 1, 2$. Therefore, q_1 is the probability that the general decision in favour of environmental taxation is taken, while q_2 is the probability that a non-uniform tax rate is introduced.

$$q_j = \frac{L_{Hj} + L_{gj}}{L_{Hj} + L_{Fj} + L_{gj}} \quad \text{with } j = 1,2 \tag{4.30}$$

with L_{Hj} and L_{Fj} denoting the lobbying contributions of U_H and U_F during stage j, and L_{gj} the Greens' fixed amount of lobbying contributions which they spend on each stage of the decision process.

The game is solved by backward induction and both firms are assumed to be risk neutral and to have perfect information.

Stage 2: Lobbying process in favour of or against a non-uniform tax rate
Again, there is a dynamic asymmetry in the game. There will only be a lobbying contest in stage 2 if there was a general decision in favour of environmental taxation during stage 1. If U_H wins in the second stage, it will earn the profit associated with a non-uniform tax rate, π_H^{nu}, which is depicted in equation 4.28. Compared to a situation with no taxes at all, U_H's profit is higher. If, however, U_H loses the second contest, it will earn the profit associated with a uniform tax rate, π^e, which is lower than in the no tax situation.[42]

U_F's situation is as follows: If a non-uniform tax rate is implemented in the second stage, the foreign firm's profit will be reduced to π_F^{nu} according to equation 4.29. This profit is lower than the profit in a situation of no taxation but it is also lower than its profit in the case of a uniform tax rate, π^e. Consequently, the firms' gains or losses from the second stage lobbying process can be written as follows with U_H's and U_F's stake on stage 2 denoted as s_H^e and s_F^e, respectively.

$$s_H^e = \pi_H^{nu} - \pi^e, \tag{4.31}$$

$$s_F^e = \pi^e - \pi_F^{nu}. \tag{4.32}$$

U_H faces the following decision problem[43]

$$\max E[\pi_{H2}] = q\,(\pi^e + s_H^e) + (1 - q)\,\pi^e - L_{H2} \tag{4.33}$$

s.t.

$$(ICC_{H2})\ \ E\big(\pi_{H2}\big)\Big|_{\substack{\text{Lobbying in} \\ \text{favour of a non} \\ \text{uniform tax rate}}} - E\big(\pi_{H2}\big)\Big|_{\substack{\text{No lobbying in} \\ \text{favour of a non} \\ \text{uniform tax rate}}} \geq 0 \tag{4.34}$$

Equation 4.34 is U_H's 'incentive compatibility constraint' to ensure that U_H's profits with lobbying are higher than without it. In other words, it has to be profitable to enter the lobbying contest.

The corresponding maximisation problem of U_F is

$$\max E[\pi_{F2}] = q\,(\pi^e - s_F^e) + (1 - q)\,\pi^e - L_{F2} \tag{4.35}$$

s.t.

$$(ICC_{F2})\ \ E\big(\pi_{F2}\big)\Big|_{\substack{\text{Lobbying against a} \\ \text{non uniform tax rate}}} - E\big(\pi_{F2}\big)\Big|_{\substack{\text{No lobbying against a} \\ \text{non uniform tax rate}}} \geq 0. \tag{4.36}$$

The contest–success function (4.31) is substituted into the firms' objective functions (4.33 and 4.35), respectively. Cournot competition leads to both competitors' optimal lobbying contributions for stage 2

$$L^*_{H2} = \frac{s_H^{e2} s_F^{e}}{\left(s_H^{e} + s_F^{e}\right)^2} - L_{g2},$$ (4.37)

$$L^*_{F2} = \frac{s_H^{e} s_F^{e2}}{\left(s_H^{e} + s_F^{e}\right)^2}.$$ (4.38)

The optimum values of both firms' expected profit functions can be derived by substituting both firms' optimum lobbying contributions, given by the equations 4.37 and 4.38, into the firms' objective functions, depicted in the equations 4.33 and 4.35. This yields

$$E[\pi_{H2}]^* = \pi^e + \frac{s_H^{e3}}{\left(s_H^{e} + s_F^{e}\right)^2} + L_{g2},$$ (4.33')

$$E[\pi_{F2}]^* = \pi^e - \frac{s_H^{e} s_F^{e}\left(s_H^{e} + 2s_F^{e}\right)}{\left(s_H^{e} + s_F^{e}\right)^2}.$$ (4.35')

Result 1:
(a) *In the second stage of the process, the public-good nature of the contested prize leads to a reduction of U_H's lobbying contributions. Its lobbying outlays are reduced exactly by the fixed amount the Greens spend in the lobbying process. Consequently, the probability of implementing the new regulation remains unchanged compared to a scenario with environmentalists making no lobbying efforts.*

(b) *In stage 2, U_F has always an incentive to participate in the game. U_H will have an incentive to spend resources on lobbying if the Greens' fixed lobbying outlays are smaller than those U_H would spend in a situation with no support from the environmentalists. In other words, due to the Nash equilibrium concept there is an optimal amount of lobbying contributions which supporters of non-uniform taxation are willing to spend. If the Greens' fixed outlays are smaller than these optimal outlays, U_H will pay the difference between the optimal outlays and the Greens' fixed contributions.*

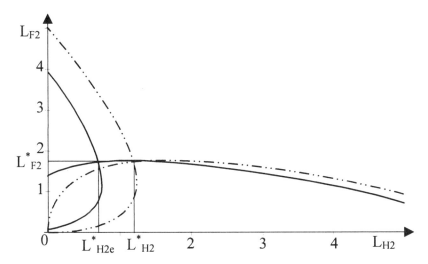

Figure 4.6 The introduction of an environmental tax – the lobbying contest in stage 2

Result 1(a) is illustrated in figure 4.6 which displays both firms' reaction functions in the case of no lobbying contributions by the environmentalists and fixed lobbying contributions by the Greens (continuous and dotted printed curves, respectively). It can easily be seen that U_F's optimal lobbying contributions ($L*_{F2}$) are unchanged. U_H's equilibrium contributions ($L*_{H2}$) are reduced by the environmentalists' outlays to the point $L*_{H2e}$ in figure 4.6. This leaves the total contributions of the coalition favouring a non-uniform tax rate unchanged.

The elaboration of result 1(a) is straightforward. Equation 4.37 indicates that U_H's lobbying contributions are reduced exactly by the environmentalists' fixed lobbying contribution ($\underline{L_{g2}}$). Consequently, plugging U_H's and U_F's optimal lobbying contributions into the contest–success function given by 4.30 shows that the term $\underline{L_{g2}}$ cancels out, leaving the probability q_2 unchanged compared to a setting with $\underline{L_{g2}} = 0$. The result is driven by the fact, that in equilibrium, there is an optimal amount of lobbying outlays spent jointly by all groups who favour a non-uniform tax rate, L_{j2}.[44] This is due to the fact that the implementation of the non-uniform tax has public good properties from U_H's and the Greens' point of view. This optimal amount can be easily obtained from equation 4.37 by setting $\underline{L_{g2}} = 0$:

$$L_{n2} = \frac{s_H^{e^2} s_F^{e}}{\left(s_H^{e} + s_F^{e}\right)^2} \tag{4.37'}$$

L_{n2} is independent of the player group bearing the costs for it, be it the Greens, U_H, or both jointly. With the Greens exogenously playing $\underline{L_{g2}}$, U_H will just invest the difference between the lobbying outlays it would play without the Greens' support and L_{g2}.

Result 1(b) can be proven as follows. U_H will always be better off if L_{n2} is spent in favour of a non-uniform tax rate in the lobbying process. U_H's profit without any lobbying in favour of the non-uniform tax are equal to π^e because, in this case, a uniform tax rate will definitely be implemented. Plugging U_H's expected profit from lobbying known from equation (4.33'), and π^e as profit in the no-lobbying case into U_H's incentive compatibility constraint yields

$$\frac{s_H^{e^3}}{\left(s_H^e + s_F^e\right)^2} + \underline{L_{g2}} \geq 0. \qquad (4.34')$$

Hence, with s_H^e and s_F^e unambiguously positive and the Greens' lobbying contributions between zero and L_{n2}, U_H will always join the contest.

U_F will always spend the lobbying contributions. Without lobbying, it will definitely face π_F^{nu}, which is equal to $\pi^e - s_F^e$. If it tries to prevent the implementation of the non-uniform tax rate by entering the lobbying contest, its expected profit will be $E[\pi_{F2}]^*$, given by 4.35'. Substituting both values into U_F's incentive compatibility constraint leads to

$$\pi^e - \frac{s_H^e \, s_F^e \left(s_H^e + 2s_F^e\right)}{\left(s_H^e + s_F^e\right)^2} \geq \pi^e - s_F^e. \qquad (4.36')$$

This is always fulfilled because s_F^e is unambiguously non-negative.

Stage 1: Introducing environmental taxation

At this stage, the general decision is made whether or not an environmental tax will be introduced. If no tax is implemented, both firms will earn normal duopoly profits, π^D. This can be derived from the equations 4.28 and 4.29 by setting the tax rates equal to zero ($t = t_H = t_F = 0$). If, however, the lobbying process in stage 1 leads to the introduction of an environmental tax, both firms will earn the expected profits determined in stage 2. They are given by the equations 4.33' and 4.35'.

For simplicity, the second term of U_H's expected profit is denoted by s_α and the second term of U_F's expected profits by s_β. Hence 4.33' and 4.35' can be re-written as

$$E[\pi_{H2}]^* = \pi^e + s_\alpha, \qquad (4.33'')$$

$$E[\pi_{F2}]^* = \pi^e - s_\beta, \qquad (4.35'')$$

with

$$s_\alpha = \frac{s_H^{e^3}}{\left(s_H^e + s_F^e\right)^2} + L_{g2}, \qquad (4.39)$$

$$s_\beta = \frac{s_H^e s_F^e \left(s_H^e + 2 s_F^e\right)}{\left(s_H^e + s_F^e\right)^2}. \qquad (4.40)$$

Furthermore, the difference between both firms' expected profits under a uniform tax rate $[\pi^e]$ and the duopoly profit without any tax, π^D, are equal to

$$s_e = \pi^D - \pi^e. \qquad (4.41)$$

This leads to U_H's maximisation problem in stage 1[45]

$$\max E[\pi_{H1}] = \pi^D + q\,(s_\alpha - s_e) - L_{H1}, \qquad (4.42)$$

s.t.

$$(ICC_{H1})\ \ E\big(\pi_{H1}\big)\Big|_{\substack{\text{Lobbying in favour} \\ \text{of environmental} \\ \text{taxation}}} \geq E\big(\pi_{H1}\big)\Big|_{\substack{\text{No lobbying in favour} \\ \text{of environmental} \\ \text{taxation}}}. \qquad (4.43)$$

while U_F is confronted with

$$\max E[\pi_{F1}] = \pi^D - q\,(s_\beta + s_e) - L_{F1}, \qquad (4.44)$$

s.t.

$$(ICC_{F1})\ \ E\big(\pi_{F1}\big)\Big|_{\substack{\text{Lobbying against} \\ \text{environmental} \\ \text{taxation}}} \geq E\big(\pi_{F1}\big)\Big|_{\substack{\text{No lobbying against} \\ \text{environmental} \\ \text{taxation}}}. \qquad (4.45)$$

The contest–success function, given by equation 4.30, is the same for both periods. U_H and U_F simultaneously decide on their lobbying contributions in stage 1. Their optimal lobbying outlays can be described as

$$L^*_{H1} = \frac{(s_e - s_\alpha)^2 (s_e + s_\beta)}{(s_\alpha + s_\beta)^2} - L_{g1}, \qquad (4.46)$$

$$L^*_{F1} = \frac{(s_\beta + s_e)^2 (s_\alpha - s_e)}{(s_\alpha + s_\beta)^2}. \qquad (4.47)$$

Substituting 4.46 and 4.47 in 4.30 yields

$$q^*_1 = \frac{s_\alpha - s_e}{s_\alpha + s_\beta}. \qquad (4.30'')$$

Result 2:
(a) *The Greens' lobbying contributions spent in favour of environmental taxation in the general decision process (stage 1) do not increase the probability of implementing the tax. These lobbying outlays nevertheless reduce the share of the optimal lobbying outlays in favour of environmental taxation paid by U_H. By this, U_H's expected profits are increased.*
(b) *The environmentalists' lobbying outlays in stage 2 (design of the tax) increase the probability of implementing the tax in stage 1 (general decision on the introduction of the environmental tax).*

Result 2(a) follows the same argumentation used to explain the similar effect on stage 2.[46]
The elaboration of result 2(b) is straightforward. As explained in result 1(a), the Greens' lobbying contributions during the second stage do not influence the probability of implementing a non-uniform tax rate. However, if the Greens set $\underline{L_{g2}} > 0$, they will pay a share of the optimal lobbying contributions in favour of this regulation $[L_{2n}]$. In the explanation of result 1, it became clear that U_H always has an incentive to pay the difference between L_{2n} and $\underline{L_{g2}}$ as long as $\underline{L_{g2}}$ is smaller than L_{2n}. By this, U_H's expected profit in stage 2, given by equation (4.33'), rises for all values of $0 < \underline{L_{g2}} < L_{n2}$ because it reduces U_H's costs of lobbying. Technically speaking, the Greens' lobbying outlays in the second stage increase the term s_α. This in turn, increases the probability of enacting the environmental taxation in the first stage. It can easily be shown by derivation of equation (4.30'') that q_2 increases in s_α, while the derivation of s_α with respect to $\underline{L_{g2}}$ is equal to one.

4.3.3 Conclusions

In the preceding section a more realistic scenario of environmental decision making was introduced. The political process was divided up into two parts. This mirrors the fact that there is one general decision in favour of or against environmental taxation made in parliament in the light of open public debate. However, questions concerning the design of the measure are frequently technical and decided upon at a committee level, which does not attract a great deal of media attention.

The Greens played an important role within this framework. Although lobbying in favour of the introduction of the environmental tax in stage 1 was 'in vain', they could influence the probability indirectly. By siding with U_H in stage 2, they increased U_H's expected profits and, via this mechanism, they raised the probability of environmental taxation implementation in the first place. In other words, non-uniform taxation will become more likely if the Greens support the protectionist interest. In turn, environmentalists seeking stricter environmental regulation should concern themselves with the design of the measures in order to find allies in the political process. Both groups support the same policy measures for completely different reasons.

NOTES

1   See General Agreement on Tariffs and Trade (1994b).
2   Loud jets, such as the Tupolevs 134 and 154, the DC-9-32, and the Boeing 727 and 737-200 are only allowed to land during the daytime. They were also excluded from weekend landing times, as announced at the beginning of 1998. See *Tagesanzeiger* (1997, p. 5).
3   Gialloretto (1989) reports a similar example for the airport of Frankfurt/Main.
4   See *Economist* (1994, p. 65).
5   For 'final' decisions within a rent-seeking contest see Stephan and Ursprung (1998) .
6   Hirshleifer (1995, p. 168). Italics added.
7   Italics added.
8   The examples of the airports in Frankfurt and Zürich mentioned earlier in this chapter underpin the practical relevance of the dichotomous case. This practical relevance is the reason why this case is analysed in detail although, technically, the contest—success functions known from Chapter 3 are more sophisticated than the (exogenous) lobbying process used in this case. In section 4.2.3 the continuous case will be analysed which, again, uses a more sophisticated lobbying technology.
9   It should be noted that $\pi^M > 2\,\pi^D$.
10 The fixed probabilities of the implementation of stricter environmental standards can be interpreted as the degeneration of a richer lobbying process, for example, a standard lobbying function. The degeneration is due to the fact that the lobbying contributions can only be set to zero or one.
11 Hereafter, a contest with both firms setting $L_i = 1$ with $i = H, F$ will be called a 'two-sided lobbying contest'. The corresponding exogenous probability of success is p_1. Respectively, a lobbying contest with only U_H spending lobbying contributions will be called a 'one-

sided lobbying contest'. In this case, the probability of success is p_2. For any possible case $p_2 > p_1$.

12   The case that the expected profits of a firm are higher with than without lobbying is denoted by (') while the opposite case is denoted by (").

13   See appendices.

14   The constraints E1 to E11 refer to figure 4.2 and figure 4.4 and are derived in appendices 2 and 3.

15   A 'no-solution' area also exists. Only pure strategies are permitted due to the structure of the model. Hence, if both firms' best responses are not consistent with each other, it will be possible that no pure strategy equilibrium exists. In this setting this is mainly due to the fact that both firms have to decide on their lobbying contributions simultaneously. Hence, it is possible that U_F spends lobbying outlays without U_H having done so. The 'prize' of the game is a complete redistribution of U_F's market share to the domestic firm. With perfect information, U_F would never spend lobbying outlays if U_H had not done so. Thus, imperfect information can prevent the existence of pure-strategy equilibria.

16   A positive discount rate would add nothing to the results of the model. Thus, for convenience a discount rate of zero is assumed throughout the model.

17   The subgame equilibria of period 1 are derived from the euqations 4.5' to 4.16" in the appendices. In the text there are given only examples.

18   The second index indicates the period with $j = 1, 2$.

19   See appendices.

20   Column 1 indicates U_H's and U_F's respective equilibrium strategies, while the first and the second row indicate period 1 and period 2.

21   The following explanations focus on figure 4.4. The constraints E1 to E11 in the figure can be derived from the firms' 'best responses'. See appendices. The interpretation of the 'no-equilibrium' area is the same as in the static case.

22   Again, the index j with $j = 1, 2$ denotes the two periods.

23   For an explanation of the 'no lobbying contest' area, see note 9.

24   The firms do not really have to be different in terms of pollution caused by production. The only requirement is that the regulation allows for discriminatory treatment. Some environmental laws, for example, distinguish between technologies according to their age, assuming that the older production process is the more polluting one. However, this assumption is not necessarily true.

25   Hereafter, it is referred to the (fixed) environmental tax simply as the 'tax'.

26   See Stephan and Ursprung (1998) for the concept of a 'final decision' in rent-seeking contests.

27   The 'economic part' of the model is similar to the one discussed in chapter 3. The profit functions in the chapters 3 and 4 are the same and are denoted by 3.4 and 3.5.

28   In contrast to chapter 3 the focus of the analysis in chapter 4 is shifted from the properties of the contest–success function to the consequences of 'final decisions' for an inter-temporal lobbying process. In order to keep the model tractable, despite the necessary extensions of the model, a standard lobbying function of the Tullock type is used instead of the more general approach used in chapter 3. The ratio function is given preference over the difference model because the Hirshleifer function always leads to 'one-sided submission'. Although, as noted earlier, there are examples for 'one-sided submission', 'two-sided lobbying contests', in the sense of different groups engaging in favour of or against new environmental standards, are the more frequent examples.

29   The numbering of the equations continues with 4.17. The equations 4.5" to 4.16' ' can be found in the appendices.

30   It should be noted that both firms' profits with $t = 0$ are, according to the equations 3.4 and 3.5, equal to the duopoly profit of a Cournot–Nash game.

31   It should be noted again that there is no discount rate. s_H and s_F are the same in both periods.

32   Differentiating 4.24 and 4.25 with respect to L_{HI} and L_{FI}, respectively, leads to the following terms

$$\frac{\partial E(\pi_{HI})}{\partial L_{HI}} = \frac{L_{FI}\, s_{II}\left(s_H^2 + 4\, s_{II}\, s_F + 2\, s_F^2\right)}{\left(L_{HI} + L_{FI}\right)^2 \left(s_H + s_F\right)^2} - 1 = 0 \text{ and } \frac{\partial E(\pi_{FI})}{\partial L_{FI}} = \frac{L_{HI}\, s_F\left(s_H^2 + 2\, s_H\, s_F + 2\, s_H^2\right)}{\left(L_{III} + L_{FI}\right)^2 \left(s_H + s_F\right)^2} - 1 = 0$$

Simultaneously solving both first-order conditions with respect to L_{HI} and L_{FI} leads to 4.26 and 4.27.

33   Only for $t > (a - b)/(2,5 + \sqrt{3})$ does $L_{HI} > L_{FI}$ follow.

34   See, for example, Hahn (1989), chapter 3 or Rauscher (1997).

35   Ursprung (1990, p. 121).

36   It should be noted that throughout this chapter the term 'tax' is interpreted as an additional constant fee per unit output.

37   In a different setting, Panagariya and Rodrik (1993) examine lobbying for a uniform or non-uniform tariff rate.

38   This assumption ensures that U_H's profits are increased and U_F's profits are decreased by the introduction of a non-uniform tax rate compared to a situation without any tax. The condition can be obtained by deducting the duopoly profit (no tax for both firms or $t_H = t_F = t$) from the profits under a non-uniform tax rate (equations 4.28 and 4.29). If a higher tax rate is applied to the foreign than to the domestic firm, this is basically a tariff.

39   The assumption of fixed lobbying outlays follows from the work of Hillman and Ursprung (1992).

40   The superscript 'nu' denotes the non-uniform tax case.

41   For a more detailed discussion see section 3.2.2.

42   As already mentioned, π^e can be derived by setting $t = t_H = t_F > 0$ in equation 4.28.

43   The first index represents the firm and the second, the stage of the decision process.

44   Again, the Greens are a member of the coalition in favour of a non-uniform tax rate because they are assumed to be interested in a reduction of the firms' joint output which can be depressed most by a non-uniform tax.

45   Equation 4.42 is a short form of U_H's maximisation problem: $E(\pi_{HI}) = q\, \pi_{H2}{}^* + (1 - q)\, \pi^D - L_{HI}$. Plugging 4.33" and 4.41 in this equation yields equation 4.42.

46   See Result 1(a).

5. The Political Economy of the US Dolphin-Safe Legislation Policy

5.1 INTRODUCTION

The first tuna–dolphin decision of the General Agreement of Tariffs and Trade (GATT) in 1991 marked the most important interface to date between liberal trade policy and environmental protection. In the US, the pro-environmental community viewed the GATT panel ruling with concern as standing in the way of a complete 'green' victory over the coalition of US canneries, fishermen from many countries and reluctant US politicians in a contest which had been ongoing for almost three decades.[1]

In 1989, the US canneries, led by Heinz, had reversed their previous re-sistance to tighter dolphin-protection standards in tuna fishing in the Eastern Tropical Pacific Ocean (ETP). They also announced that they themselves would no longer buy tuna fished in the ETP. This was a reversal of their po-sition over the previous thirty years. The new situation resulted in a signifi-cant reduction in deaths of dolphins. With the exception of Mexico and some other countries which were boycotted for not complying with the US dolphin regulation and a few San Diego-based fishermen, it seemed that every rele-vant domestic interest group had been forced into the coalition of 'Flipper's friends' by pro-dolphin sentiment.

The different possible explanations for the success of the US dolphin-safe policy in the ETP[2] are reflected in the sociology and endogenous trade-policy literature. Sociologists have pointed to the rising influence of 'Greens': Gorz (1987) and Lash and Urry (1987) claim that new green social movements succeeded in overriding labour interests as counterpart interests of large cor-porations in the political process.[3] Enlightened policies thus prevailed over narrow economic self-interest. The literature on the political economy of trade policy has, on the other hand, examined how the presence of environ-mental interest might influence the determination of trade policies. The issue here as to whether pro-environmental interest can be expected to share a common goal with interest groups seeking either a liberal trade policy or protectionist policies (see Hillman and Ursprung (1992, 1994a)), or how a politician who is using his ability to choose a policy which would be to his personal advantage might internalise the presence of environmental interests (see Aidt (1998)).

In the case of dolphin-safe tuna fishing, what appears to be complete submission of one of the private interest groups can be observed. This chapter considers whether this ostensibly conceding interest group did indeed belong to the coalition which lost due to US dolphin-safe legislation. The chapter investigates the considerations which underlie a change in the dominant US canneries' economic interests, and shows how the new dolphin-safe legislation raised domestic rivals' costs and adversely affected foreign tuna processors.

After introducing the history of the US dolphin-safe legislation in section 5.2, the key interest groups – the canneries, the fishermen, and the environmentalists – are the respective subjects of the sections 5.3–5.5. Each section contains an analysis of how economic and political factors may have influenced an interest group's position on dolphin-safe legislation prior to the policy reversal in 1989/1990. Section 5.6, summarises the course of the dolphin-safe policy from 1991 until 1997.

5.2 THE HISTORY OF THE US DOLPHIN-SAFE POLICY

The origins of the US dolphin-safe policy date back more than a quarter of a century. In 1972 the US Congress enacted the Marine Mammal Protection Act (MMPA). At that time, the stocks of the marine mammals, namely seals, sea lions, whales, porpoises, dolphins, sea otters, manatees, walruses and polar bears were steadily declining. Conservationists started a heated debate on how to protect these animals. The environmentalist pressure groups followed different approaches. Some of them argued in favour of a complete ban on killing ocean mammals, while others headed for sustainable management of the marine mammal stocks.[4] Finally, the concept of a permanent moratorium on the killing of marine mammals carried the day.

The MMPA is not only concerned with fishing operations directly targeted at marine mammals, such as whaling, commercial fishing operations which result in the incidental killing of marine mammals are also within its scope. In the Eastern Tropical Pacific Ocean, a special coexistence of tunas and dolphins is observed. Schools of tuna and dolphins swim together and fishermen have been intentionally encircling schools of dolphins to catch the tuna swimming underneath.[5] This purse seine harvesting technique, where the fishermen intentionally set on dolphins, has only been found in the ETP.[6] It was estimated that in 1973 a total of 252,000 dolphins were killed in this area.[7] The dolphin mortality can be reduced by a so-called backdown procedure which involves releasing the dolphins after the entanglement. An additional dolphin safety panel (Medina panel) can very often prevent entanglement and mortality of these dolphins during this procedure.[8]

In 1972, a two-year-exemption was made from the zero-mortality provision of the MMPA for the tuna fishermen. An amendment to require the fishermen to reach a zero-mortality of dolphins at once was not accepted in the US Senate.[9] Prior to 1976, nothing happened with respect to tuna fishing. After a lawsuit, the National Marine Fisheries Service (NMFS) issued regulations and set up a quota for dolphins that could be killed incidentally in commercial fishing operations.[10] After years of postponing the zero-mortality goal for dolphins, it was completely given up in the re-authorisation process of 1981 and was replaced by the provision that the 'safest possible technology' be used.[11] It is undisputed that the regulation, which was implemented by the NMFS, constituted an incentive for the US and foreign fleets to implement technologies that significantly decreased the dolphin mortality rate, in particular, the requirement to use a dolphin-safe panel (Medina panel) and fine nets. In addition, observer coverage by either officials of the NMFS or of the Inter-American Tropical Tuna Commission (IATTC), which has been concerned with the tuna–dolphin issue since 1977, was required. The number of dolphin deaths dropped from 252,000 in 1973 to 8,258 in 1984. Nevertheless, the actual quota of dolphins, which could be killed incidentally during the tuna harvest in the ETP, remained at 20,500 in the 1980s. Hence, the quota never constituted a binding restriction for the US fishermen. The regulations of the MMPA were designed in such a way that the US fishing fleet could further utilise the tuna resources of the ETP.[12] This pattern of legislation balancing economic and ecological concerns remained constant until the end of the 1980s.

In 1988, however, the structure of the US regulation with respect to tuna fishing in the ETP changed. The re-authorisation process of the MMPA in that year was used to prohibit the US Department of State from finding foreign dolphin protection standards comparable to the US standards, unless certain criteria were met.[13] This regulation constituted the legal base for the later embargo on Mexican tuna.

After the US government had ignored the 1988-amendments of the MMPA for a year and a half, several environmentalists headed by the California-based Earth Island Institute sued the US Department of Commerce in mid 1990 for not enforcing the MMPA with respect to imported tuna.[14] The court ordered the government to prohibit the importation of tuna harvested in the ETP with purse seines. Consequently, the US government imposed embargoes on Mexican tuna imports and imported tuna from the so-called intermediary countries.[15] In 1989/90 the Dolphin Protection Consumer Information Bill (Boxer Bill) was legislated. It basically denied the label 'dolphin-safe' to almost every tuna caught in the ETP by purse seiners. Even before the law came into force in 1990/91, the main US canneries, accounting for about 80 per cent of the US market in canned tuna,[16] declared their 'own' new dolphin-safe policy. This meant that they would not process tuna from the ETP any longer. Forcing a billion dollar industry[17] to withdraw from the ETP was seen as a major victory of the environmentalist pressure groups and it was considered to indicate the increasing strength of the Greens. The canneries' decision more or less ended the presence of large US purse seiners in the ETP, where they had fished since these ships were developed in the 1960s.

5.3 THE US CANNERIES

The US canneries are a highly concentrated industry and, hence, constitute one of the key interest groups in the political process leading to the policy change in the dolphin protection regulation between 1988 and 1990. It is therefore central to this chapter to determine why the canneries switched from lobbying against stricter dolphin protection standards to actively supporting the policy. Section 5.3.1 introduces the three 'giants' in the US tuna market, their parent companies and evaluates their political influence. Section 5.3.2 explains the canneries' changing economic interest in the ETP due to plant relocation prior to their policy change in 1989/90. Section 5.3.3 discusses the tuna embargo on Mexico as a measure which benefited the US industry by excluding a potentially highly competitive industry from the domestic market. Section 5.3.4 shows that the economic effect of the big canneries' sudden introduction of a 'new' dolphin-safe policy raised their smaller domestic rivals' costs considerably.

5.3.1 The 'Key Players'

All major US tuna canneries have been subsidiaries of larger processed food conglomerates and 'the position of the major US tuna companies on tuna issues . . . is frequently established on the basis of the broader interest of the parent companies'.[18] In the 1980s two of these canneries, Bumble Bee and van Camp, were sold abroad to powerful East-Asian food processors, which changed their economic interest in the ETP.

StarKist
Since 1963 StarKist, the largest US cannery, has been a 100 per cent subsidiary of H.J. Heinz Company, a Pennsylvania-based processed-food conglomerate. In 1990, StarKist accounted for almost one third of the US market. H.J. Heinz also owned an Australian tuna cannery which supplied the majority of that market. At the end of the 1980s, approximately 16 per cent of the world-wide sales of H.J. Heinz were related to tuna.[19] StarKist also operates a plant in Puerto Rico and the world's second largest cannery on American Samoa. The company has been active in Pago Pago since 1963. Between 1986 and 1987 StarKist and van Camp Seafood, which operates the second cannery in Pago Pago, doubled the output of canned tuna on

American Samoa.[20] This expansion offshore is remarkable because it is related to the company's divestment on the mainland. In 1984, StarKist closed its last mainland production facility on Terminal Island 'in response to continued high costs and the Government's failure to provide relief from continued low-priced canned tuna imports.'[21]

The importance of tuna for Heinz even rose after 1990. On 11 July 1996, it was announced that H.J. Heinz intended to buy the Bumble Bee canneries in Puerto Rico and Ecuador, as well as the loining plant in Santa Fe Springs, California.[22]

Bumble Bee

In 1990, Bumble Bee was the second largest US tuna cannery and accounted for approximately 23 per cent of the US market. It has canned tuna since 1937 and expanded substantially in the late 1970s and early 1980s when it belonged to Castle and Cook.[23] In 1985, when its parent company was in financial difficulties, the managers purchased the firm in a leveraged buyout[24] and sold it three years later. After only one year of being a subsidiary of the Pillsbury Company, a US food processor, Bumble Bee was purchased in 1989 for US$ 269 million by the Thai Unicord group, which belongs to a larger conglomerate owned by the Thai Konnutakiet family. Unicord is an agribusiness conglomerate which has become one of the world's largest tuna packers. Unicord had long-term contracts with suppliers from Japan, Taiwan, the US, the Maldives, Papua New Guinea and the Solomon Islands. Unicord owns considerable tuna canning facilities in Thailand and, through Bumble Bee, a cannery in Puerto Rico, a loining plant[25] in California and a plant in Ecuador.[26] Unicord sells canned tuna under the 'Bumble Bee' label from its own US facilities as well as from its plants abroad. In 1990, 48 per cent of Unicord's canned tuna production was exported to the US, another 35 per cent to Europe and 8 per cent to Japan. Although, the Bumble Bee purchase helped to cut costs by circumventing US import duties,[27] Unicord ran into financial difficulties after the buyout.[28] Despite all efforts of consolidation in the early 1990s, Unicord sold the Bumble Bee plants to StarKist in 1996.[29]

Van Camp

Van Camp Seafood is the third largest tuna cannery in the US and accounted for almost 20 per cent of the US market in 1990. It sells tuna under the label 'Chicken of the Sea'. Until 1988 van Camp was owned by Ralston Purina, a large US food processor, and accounted for approx. 7 per cent of its parent company's total sales in 1987.[30] In 1988 it was bought for US$ 260 million by P.T. Management Trust (Mantrust), a privately held Indonesian group with substantial interests in agribusiness. In 1988, van Camp Seafood owned a cannery on American Samoa, one in Puerto Rico and jointly possessed a factory in Bali with the US Tunafleet Cooperative Association.[31] By 1984 van Camp ended its engagement on mainland US by closing its tuna factory in

San Diego, which was said to be the most modern in the world.[32] In 1990, during the hearing on the Boxer Bill, it announced that it would close its plant in Puerto Rico. Mantrust did not only sell canned tuna under the 'Chicken of the Sea' label, which originated in the US, but also products canned in its plants in Indonesia.

On 12 April 1990, these three influential companies announced their decision not to buy tuna from the ETP any longer. This 'new' policy was welcomed in the US Congress which was in the process of discussing the International Dolphin Protection Consumer Information Act. It solved the politicians' conflict over how to balance ecological and economic interests. The canneries' policy reversal left the tuna fishermen alone to resist stricter dolphin protection laws.[33] Nevertheless, the canneries' motives were questioned. Rep. Studds summarised the concerns in the hearing on the Boxer Bill when he asked Dan Sullivan, the CEO of Bumble Bee: 'The tuna controversy has been around 20 years, Chicken of the Sea and Bumble Bee have been buying unsafe tuna for more than 20 years, animals groups have been unhappy about that for more than 20 years, tuna consumption went up last year . . . so what happened?'[34] Anthony J.F. O'Reilly, the CEO of Heinz, claimed that the decision was caused by 'epic debate almost theological in tone.'[35] and wrote to Barbara Boxer, the sponsor of the new act, that '[t]he leadership shown by you . . . was an important consideration in the adoption of our policy.'[36] It was widely argued by the public that the consumer boycott which David Phillips, the director of the California-based Earth Island Institute, threatened to renew was an important reason for the companies to change their policy.[37] Nevertheless, internal marketing surveys of Heinz showed that only half of all consumers were willing to pay for dolphin-safe tuna.[38] In addition, consumer boycotts were already in place in 1988 when the tuna consumption peaked.[39] The data concerning the per capita consumption of tuna peaked in 1989 shortly before the US canneries announced their retreat from the ETP as shown in table 5.1.

The figure declined in 1990, after the new policy was in place. It is hard to see any positive short-term impact of the dolphin-safe issue on US tuna consumption.

In the remainder of section 5.3, the economic impact the proposed regulation and the canneries' policy change had the tuna processing industry will be analysed more thoroughly.

Table 5.1 US annual per capita consumption of canned tuna, 1975–95

Year	Tuna*	Year	Tuna*
1975	2.9	1986	3.6
1976	2.8	1987	3.5
1977	2.8	1988	3.6
1978	3.3	1989	3.9
1979	3.2	1990	3.7
1980	3.0	1991	3.6
1981	3.0	1992	3.5
1982	2.8	1993	3.5
1983	3.2	1994	3.3
1984	3.2	1995	3.4
1985	3.3		

Note: * measured in pounds

Source: US National Marine Fisheries Service (1995): *Fisheries of the United States.*

5.3.2 Explaining the Plant Relocation in the 1980s

Prior to the 1980s almost all of the US tuna canneries were located in south-ern California close to the ETP. During the 1950s, US tuna companies had built only a few canning facilities on Puerto Rico.[40] But from 1979–85, in just six years, the US canneries closed all of their mainland production facilities with one exception.[41] In 1990, just a few weeks after introducing their new dolphin-safe policy, van Camp Seafood closed its tuna factory in Ponce, Puerto Rico. Table 5.2 shows the canneries' relocation.

Table 5.2 does not give a complete picture of the movement offshore because, although the number of canneries on American Samoa remained constant, the capacity rose considerably. In 1988 the StarKist cannery on American Samoa reported a daily raw fish packing capacity of 900,000 pounds, which made it the second largest cannery in the world.[42]

American Samoa and Puerto Rico together accounted for 93 per cent of the commercial tuna landings of the US.[43] American tuna canneries, StarKist Samoa and VCS Samoa Packing (then van Camp) had been active on Ameri-can Samoa since 1963. However, between 1986 and 1987, they expanded their capacities from 9,709,000 to 18,742,000 cases. Thus, the export of canned tuna almost doubled. Another sharp increase occurred between 1990 and 1991 from 15,252,000 to 26,269,000 cases. Table 5.3 illustrates the expansion of tuna exports from American Samoa.

Table 5.2 The canneries' location, 1980–90

Plant location	1980	1985	1986	1987	1988	1989	1990
Continental US	12	1	1	1	1	1	2*
Puerto Rico	5	5	5	5	5	5	3
American Samoa	2	2	2	2	2	2	2
Hawaii	1	0	0	0	0		0
	20	8	8	8	8	8	7

Note: * Bumble Bee opened a plant for loining in Santa Fe Springs in 1990.

Source: US International Trade Commission (1992, p. D12).

Table 5.3 American Samoa: exports of canned tuna, 1977–93

Year	Thousands of cases	Value (US$ 1,000)	Year	Thousands of cases	Value (US$ 1,000)
1977	2,814	73,098	1985	6,989	187,497
1978	3,238	96,823	1986	9,709	225,746
1979	3,962	120,804	1987	18,742	268,645
1980	4,094	120,278	1988	14,067	354,842
1981	5,183	190,382	1989	15,671	296,594
1982	5,419	181,782	1990	15,252	296,559
1983	5,563	166,870	1992	26,269	303,204
1984	8,190	202,405	1993	31,600	484,640

Source: American Samoa Government (1994): *Statistical Digest.*

The reasons for this massive relocation fall within three categories: labour costs, government intervention and the availability of raw tuna.

Labour costs
Although labour is a relatively small item in the total cost of production, certain important stages of the tuna canning process, in particular the cleaning of the fish, are highly labour intensive. However, for 1989/90 the wage rates shown in table 5.4, were compiled by the International Trade Commission.[44]

The cost advantage of American Samoa has remained constant. Even in 1996 the average hourly wage rate of the cannery workers was US$ 3.73 which was 63 cents above the minimum wage rate on American Samoa.[45] Nevertheless, although these data show a big cost advantage for American Samoa, it has to be taken into account that these benefits from producing offshore are partly offset by higher transportation costs to the important canned tuna markets on the US mainland. Several measures, including downsizing and relocation, enabled the US canneries (including the smaller companies) to considerably reduce the relative and absolute cost of labour in the canning process as shown in table 5.5.[46]

Table 5.4 Average wage rates per hour including fringe benefits in the US canneries in 1989

	Wage rates
Mainland US	12 US$
Puerto Rico	7.47 US$ (minimum wage)
American Samoa	3.40 US$

Source: US International Trade Commission (1990, p. 2.18).

Table 5.5 US processors' costs of direct labour in operations producing canned tuna for human consumption

Year	Cost of direct labour (US$ million)	Costs of direct labour as percentage of the total production costs
1979	72.8	10.2
1980	66.2	9.5
1981	79.5	9.3
1982	73.0	9.1
1983	81.0	10.4
1984	69.3	10.0
1985	51.5	7.8
1986	73.4	8.4
1987	83.7	8.7
1988	83.5	8.0
1989	79.7	7.6
1990	66.2	6.4
1991	61.1	6.1

Source: US International Trade Commission (1992, p. D23)

Governmental regulation

Territories currently favoured by the US canneries, Puerto Rico and American Samoa, enjoy various benefits,[47] which provide an incentive to locate plants in both places. According to Section 936 of the Internal Revenue Act,[48] a domestic corporation is allowed a tax credit equal to the taxable income from the active conduct of a trade or business within a possession of the US.[49] 'Thus income derived from possessions in Puerto Rico and American Samoa is effectively exempted from the US corporate income tax.'[50] In addition, both American Samoa and Puerto Rico provide extensive exemptions from their own taxes. The two big canneries in American Samoa have enjoyed such benefits since 1985. Puerto Rico has granted a similar scheme of exemptions for ten to 25 years, the amount of exemptions decreasing with time. American Samoa, in particular, has always been interested in providing the canneries with favourable economic conditions because almost 30 per cent of the total workforce have been employed by the canneries since the expansion of the facilities to the island.[51]

Furthermore, the harbour of American Samoa in Pago Pago is exempt from the Nicholson Act. Hence, it is the only US port where foreign fishermen are allowed to land fish without being forced to bear high transshipment costs from harbours outside the US. Former US vessels fishing in the Western Tropical Pacific, for example, which were sold to a foreign flag can still directly supply the US canneries in American Samoa.

Although American Samoa is located outside the US customs area, exports of canned tuna into the US are not dutiable. However, relocating to these islands has the favourable side effect for the US firms that their foreign competitors have to bear a higher average tariff rate. The US tariff for canned tuna in brine[52] is split: 6 per cent ad valorem for packs under the quota, 12.5 per cent for shipments above it. The quota is recalculated each year and equals 20 per cent of each year's domestic production. For the canneries located outside the US customs area, canned tuna in brine from American Samoa does not count for the quota.[53] By this mechanism, the relocation of production capacity to American Samoa reduces the quota of canned tuna which may be imported into the US at the tariff rate of 6 per cent.

Supply of tuna

Availability of raw tuna Apart from the wage rates, the costs and availability of raw tuna play a key role for the location of the canneries. Raw tuna accounts for the bulk of the canneries' costs. In 1990, 69.9 per cent of the firms' total costs were attributed to the purchase of raw tuna as shown in table 5.6.

In the decades until the 1980s, the US tuna canneries had difficulties in ensuring the supply of fresh tuna for their canneries on the world market. Hence, for both the US tuna fleet and the canneries, vertical integration was a beneficial arrangement. Most of the tuna boats were either owned directly by the canneries or at least financed by them. That helped the vessel owners to raise the high investment requirement of US$ 5 million to US$ 15 million per vessel. The canneries ensured a steady supply of raw and frozen tuna for their processing plants with this arrangement.[54]

Table 5.6   US processors' costs of raw tuna in operations producing canned tuna for human consumption

Year	Cost of raw tuna (US$ million)	Costs of raw tuna as percentage of the total production costs
1980	481.3	69.0
1981	603.8	70.9
1982	544.6	67.6
1983	491.2	63.1
1984	421.5	60.7
1985	366.8	55.7
1986	531.3	60.8
1987	591.6	61.3
1988	690.2	66.3
1989	680.3	64.9
1990	725.1	69.9
1991	727.1	72.3

Source: US International Trade Commission (1992, p. D23).

The US tuna vessel owners have always been a dispersed group. Until the end of the 1980s, however, the harvesting sector could be regarded as highly concentrated because the marketing representation for almost half of the US tuna vessels was provided by the American Tuna Sales Association (ATSA) which negotiated the prices with the canneries. Until that time, the prices negotiated by the ATSA had been fairly representative even for non-ATSA-members. This originally mutually beneficial relationship came to an end when imported tuna became more available in the US. This was due to expansion of the foreign fleets[55] as well as the development of new fishing grounds. Tuna fishing was introduced in the Indian Ocean[56] and more tuna was caught in the Western Tropical Pacific Ocean (WTP).

Figure 5.1[57] illustrates the rapid growth of the fisheries in the Indian Ocean, which accounted for almost a third of the world's total tuna catches.[58] As a result, the tuna canneries cut their close links to the tuna harvesting sector.

One result of this dissolution of the vertical integration in the tuna industry was that the canneries' interest in the US fleet decreased. After reducing their involvement in the harvesting sector, there was little incentive left for the canneries to engage in lobbying against stricter dolphin protection standards.

They were able to purchase tuna from other sources (including US vessels which had moved to the Western Tropical Pacific). Furthermore, the canneries could relocate their production facilities without considering the fishermen's interests – they had to undertake considerable investments to upgrade or replace their purse seiners in order to shift to the WTP.[59] Hence, the opportunity to divest in the tuna harvesting sectors removed another obstacle for moving canneries offshore and utilising tax benefits and cheaper labour there.

Figure 5.1 Tuna catches by ocean

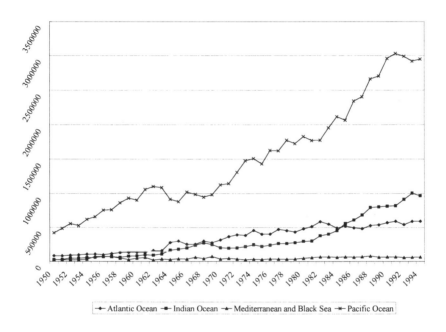

Source: FAO (1995): *Fisheries Statistics – Catches and Landings*

Basically, two means of supply were available to the US tuna processing sector apart from the US fleet. Imported tuna could be purchased and transhipped to the US, or tuna from foreign flag vessels could be unloaded in the port of Pago Pago on American Samoa, the only US harbour exempted from the Nicholson Act which prohibits foreign flag vessels from landing tuna directly in a US port. The greater availability of tuna in the world market did not, of course, necessarily mean that the actual US imports rose each year. The US tuna canneries could, however, abandon their safeguards in the form of vertical integration with the tuna fleet for ensuring a steady supply of raw fish. In case of a shortage, the companies could now rely on the world market. At the end of 1985, van Camp held equity in 15 purse seiners, eight of which it completely owned and one of which it leased.[60] All vessels were sold in the following years.

By 1981, van Camp Seafood had already decreased its reliance on tuna from the Eastern Tropical Pacific. On 29 June, 1990 van Camp closed its factory in Puerto Rico, which was 'an economic issue, and the dolphin announcement merely accelerated our decision to close the cannery'.[61] For van Camp, this was the last step of divestment in the ETP. With abundant raw tuna in the world market, van Camp no longer held major stakes in this ocean. StarKist held no equity in vessels in the ETP and its plant in Puerto Rico also served to process Atlantic tuna, which is not associated with dolphins.

A backdoor to the 'Fortress America'   Both foreign owned canneries, van Camp and Bumble Bee, also use raw tuna supplied by their parent companies. Foreign competitors face a high tariff of 36 per cent on tuna packed in oil. The tariff for tuna packed in brine is split: 6 per cent for tuna under the import quota,[62] 12 per cent for tuna above it. The Indonesian P.T. Mantrust, through its subsidiary van Camp Seafood, avoids these tariffs by way of its American Samoa cannery, where they can land – thanks to the exemption from the Nicholson Act – foreign flag tuna directly. The Thai Unicord group took a different route. By acquiring Bumble Bee it countered 'the stiff US tariffs and quotas on imports of canned tuna to protect Unicord's stake in the US market'.[63] Prepared tuna or loins are just charged with a 1.1 per cent tariff. Bumble Bee's California plant just processes frozen loins, while the cannery on Puerto Rico processes loins and fresh tuna alike. Apart from circumventing the US tariffs 'the strategy ensures a place in US grocery stores for both their acquired and their own products, it consolidates the competition, and not least it retains the Asian suppliers the profits from the cannery to the check-out line'.[64]

5.3.3 The Tuna Embargo

Factual aspects
In 1984, the US Congress amended the MMPA to allow embargoes on tuna from countries which employed 'less protective' dolphin-safe measures than the US.[65] In 1988, specific rules for implementing these provisions were legislated.[66] 'The 1988 amendments to the MMPA set in place a rigid comparability test between the kills-per-set (KPS) by the US fleet and the kills-per-set by foreign fleets. If the comparability test is not met, or the other rules are not observed, then non-discretionary trade embargoes are imposed – these embargoes relate to yellowfin tuna caught in the eastern tropical Pacific Ocean.'[67] The American Tunaboat Association fleet held a general permit allowing for a quota of up to 20,500 incidental dolphin deaths per year due to US tuna fishing. The foreign fleets were required not to exceed 2 times and 1.25 times the US rate in 1989 and 1990, respectively. Furthermore, the 1988

amendments and the implementation regulations issued by the National Oce-anic and Atmospheric Administration (NOAA) contained specific obligations which must be met by any country in order to export yellowfin tuna from the ETP to the US.[68] In October 1990, the US Department of Commerce was forced by a court order[69] to impose embargoes on tuna imports from Mexico and other countries. Despite two panel decisions of the General Agreement on Tariffs and Trade (GATT)[70] against the US, the embargo against Mexico continued until the end of the 1990s.

However, by 1992, the US Department of State reported that Mexico had already undertaken serious attempts to decrease the dolphin mortality. The number of killed dolphins per set reduced from 8.2 in 1988 to 4.8 in 1990, when the embargo was imposed and further decreased to 2.9 in 1991. In 1991, the Mexican fishermen achieved a rate of killed dolphins per set below that of the US fleet in 1988 when the embargo provisions were introduced into the MMPA. Nevertheless, the trade restrictions were not lifted because the number of killed dolphins per set of the US fleet had decreased even fur-ther, in particular because, in 1990, the US purse seiner fleet had almost en-tirely left the ETP. With the number of Mexican purse seiners only slightly decreasing from 49 in 1988 to 43 in 1991, the provision of the MMPA[71] could hardly be met by the Mexican fishermen despite all their efforts.[72]

The US canneries' interest in the tuna embargo

The MMPA embargo provision of 1988 was supported by a broad coalition of interest groups, such as US fishermen, environmentalists and the US can-neries. The American Tuna Foundation representing the American tuna in-dustry in the tuna dolphin controversy strongly advocated import regulations in Congress hearings.[73]

> The US tuna industry believes that the import regulations of March 18, 1988 were long overdue. We have consistently asserted the need to examine the incidental take of marine mammals by foreign purse seine vessels operating in the ETP ocean tuna fishery . . . We share the concern of other interested parties over the fact that implementation of the import regulation was delayed for such an excessive pe-riod.[74]

This statement illustrates a policy change of the big canneries. In the 1970s and the beginning of the 1980s, they advocated more strongly measures which could ensure their tuna supply from the ETP. This 'new' attitude to the problem was driven by two forces. On the one hand, the greater availability of raw tuna in the world market and the resulting divestment of the canneries in vessels and canning facilities made them less dependent on raw tuna from the ETP. On the other hand, the rapidly growing Mexican tuna industry just across the border made the market for canned tuna much more competitive, in turn making trade barriers, from the US canneries' point of view, much more desirable.

Raw tuna A document of the National Marine Fisheries Service (NMFS)[75] points out that import restrictions for tuna from the ETP in the early 1980s might have resulted in a shortage of raw products and loss of considerable investments in ETP countries.

However, by the end of the 1980s, the situation had changed considerably. The development of tuna fishing in other regions, notably the Indian Ocean and the Western Tropical Pacific Ocean, had increased the world tuna supply. Consequently, the US companies had sold off their equity in the ETP fishing vessels and reduced the size of their production facilities in this region if they did not need it for processing tuna from outside the region.[76] Furthermore, a lot of US vessels had already shifted to the Western Pacific Ocean where they now supplied the canneries on American Samoa. Hence, there was no fear of a tuna shortage for the large canneries. They could easily buy on the world market.

Canned tuna When the US canneries lost their interest in the ETP as a source of raw tuna, Mexico was about to become a serious competitor for the US companies in their domestic market for canned tuna.

In the mid 1980s, the Latin American fishing industry accounted for approximately 20 per cent of the total world catches.[77] With respect to tuna, Mexico had become the leading fishing country in this region. The number of vessels had increased significantly over the decades and peaked in 1986 with 98 vessels,[78] all of which mainly operated in the ETP. Although the number of vessels did not meet the fleet size aimed at in the Mexican tuna development plan of 1977, by the mid 1980s, the fleet was the second largest in the region, second only to that of the United States. From 1980 to 1988 the Mexican tuna landings increased from 34,429 to 135,620 short tons. Furthermore, the Mexican tuna industry did not have to rely on outside assistance because there is abundant tuna within the 200-mile Economic exclusive zone, 75 per cent of which is off the coast of Baja California, close to most of the Mexican canning facilities.[79] According to Hudgins (1987), the Mexican government has actively supported the expansion of the tuna industry by direct ownership of tuna vessels and some production facilities, as well as by tax benefits and political measures. At the end of the 1980s, the Mexican state owned 22 per cent of the tuna vessels and supported investment and the daily business of the harvesting and processing sector by loans from the state-owned Banco Nacional Pesquero y Portuario.

The most important harbour for tuna is Ensenada in Baja California Norte.[80] At the end of the 1980s, the Mexican government set up a programme to improve its facilities.[81] Before this programme, Mexico suffered from serious problems such as too little refrigeration capacity and quality problems. Serious efforts were made to improve the situation.[82] Most canneries are located close to the main US markets for canned tuna with extremely low transportation costs compared to the US competitors offshore.

Further the canneries in Baja California and Ensenada enjoy the status of a free-trade zone. This has been very favourable for the Mexican producers because, with a relatively small domestic market, the state-supported expansion of the Mexican tuna industry clearly aimed at the US markets.

However, the US closed its market for Mexican tuna products from 14 July 1980 through August 1986 with an embargo imposed under the Magnuson Fishery Conservation and Management Act of 1979 (MFCMA).[83] The reason for the embargo was a long-standing disagreement among the US and other countries about control and access to tuna resources. Since the development of purse seiners in the 1950s, US tuna vessels had started to harvest tuna almost everywhere off Central and South America. After extending the fishing zones from three or 12 miles to 200 miles, conflicts arose because the US did not recognise the countries' jurisdiction over tuna. On the one hand, the US argument that tuna is highly migratory and, hence, cannot be effectively managed by an individual nation has some merits. On the other hand, following this line of argument benefited the US economically because American vessels could enter the major tuna grounds while in turn hardly any tuna can be found in the US EEZ.[84] This conflict led to frequent seizures of US vessels. Under the MFCMA, the US fishermen were insured against these seizures and, furthermore, fish products from countries taking US vessels could be embargoed. The conflict concerning tuna intensified when problems of overfishing arose in the ETP. In 1979, the members of the Inter-American Tropical Tuna Commission were unable to agree on an extension of the conservation measures for yellowfin tuna, which had been in place since 1966.[85] Efforts to negotiate the access to Mexican waters bilaterally failed in 1980. In the same year, the US put the embargo under the MFCMA in place. 'In Mexico City the "tuna war" with the United States was seen as an issue of national integrity, while enforcement of the US embargo was primarily motivated by domestic protectionism.'[86] The complaint about protectionism might not be entirely misleading because it is believed that the Mexican proposal of a voluntary export restraint of 20,000 tons in April 1986 made the resolution of the conflict in August of the same year possible. Nevertheless, the US market was open for Mexican tuna only until 1990 when a court order forced the US Department of Commerce to embargo Mexico under the MMPA because of the tuna–dolphin problem.[87]

In effect, first the embargo under the Magnuson Act and later under the MMPA protected the US canneries from Mexican exports. These exports might have become a threat to the US canneries because of lower transportation costs to the major US market, compared to the canned tuna from American Samoa and Puerto Rico, cheap labour and Mexican government support. The closing of the US market for Mexican products might have contributed to the profitability of the US investments, in particular, on American Samoa. Thus, the decreasing dependency of the US canneries on raw tuna from the ETP coupled with the threat the expanding Mexican tuna industry constituted for their domestic market in canned tuna made the US canneries' support for the embargo economically perfectly rational.

5.3.4 Raising Rivals' Costs – the Little Canneries

Apart from the arguments raised thus far and the fact that the 'dolphin-safe' label is a powerful marketing tool, there is another domestic reason for the support of these measures. By lobbying in favour of tighter environmental regulation, the big canneries could substantially weaken their smaller US rivals.[88]

In 1990, the US International Trade Commission noted the following regarding the US market: 'Six US processors of canned tuna currently account for the vast majority of US production . . . The three largest firms, accounting for about 80 per cent of domestic production of canned tuna in 1989, are StarKist Seafood Company, Bumble Bee Seafoods, and van Camp Seafood.'[89] Nineteen per cent of the market belonged to three smaller canneries: Pan Pacific, Caribe and Neptune. The remaining one per cent of the market consisted of small food-processing companies which were producing on an irregular basis.[90] The announcement of the three big canneries not to buy tuna from the ETP any longer made it almost impossible for other firms to sell dolphin-unsafe tuna. Obviously, the smaller companies were surprised by this policy change. While the three larger canneries announced their policy change on 12 April 1990, Caribe, for example, was only able to follow on 25 April 1990[91] when it became obvious that there was no longer a market for dolphin-unsafe tuna in the US. Hence, the smaller canneries had to switch to different sources of raw tuna, either from outside the ETP, or from baitboats, longliners or small purse seiners in the ETP. All of them employ dolphin-safe harvesting techniques which are not very productive. Switching the sources of the major factor of production in the middle of the harvesting season within one week imposed high costs on the little canneries which had to follow the 'new' dolphin-safe policy. However, being forced to switch to less-productive sources was financially disastrous.

Neptune Packing was a subsidiary of the Japanese Mitsui group and operated a plant in Puerto Rico. The parent company decided to close the cannery in Ponce in August of the same year.

Caribe, a subsidiary of the Japanese Mitsubishi holding also owned a tuna cannery in Puerto Rico. 'Caribe is a relatively small participant and is more vulnerable to shifts in raw material supplies and prices than its larger competitors are, since it traditionally has lower volume requirements and has purchased more on the spot market.'[92] In 1990, the company started to utilise loins, prepared tuna, from Ecuador in response to higher labour costs and the reduced availability of tuna from the ETP.

Among the smaller canneries, Pan Pacific, a subsidiary of Marifarms, was the only company which had remained on the mainland US in Terminal Island/California where almost all tuna processors were originally located. The company tried to utilise the advantage of low transportation costs to the Californian market for canned tuna. However, Pan Pacific suffered from the high costs of labour in California, and consequently, employment fell from 1,228 workers in 1984 to 525 workers in 1989. Pan Pacific traditionally used raw tuna from the local fleet in the ETP or its own vessels.[93] After the big canneries' dolphin-safe decision, Pan Pacific tried to secure its supply by buying tuna from baitboats in the ETP. However, this strategy failed because of the US embargo on Mexico and the recognition of the 200 mile Economic exclusive zone (EEZ) by the US administration in 1990. Baitboats had to rely heavily on tuna from Mexican waters. When the US changed the Magnuson Act in 1992 and recognised the national jurisdiction over tuna in the 200 mile EEZ, the US fishing vessels lost their protection and insurance against seizure by the Mexican government. In an International Trade Commission hearing on 4 February 1992, the president of the Western Fishboat Owners Association testified that without access to Mexican waters, the US baitboat fleet would be unable to supply a sufficient quantity of raw tuna to Pan Pacific.[94] The company also reported that an access agreement with Mexico would support the local Californian baitboats, longline fleet and purse seiners under 400 tons and, furthermore, ensure Pan Pacific's supply of raw tuna. But with the tuna embargo on Mexico in place, the Mexican government refused to negotiate a new treaty.[95] In summer 1995, Pan Pacific went bankrupt owing more than US$ 7 million to its creditors and leaving its workers unemployed.[96] It claimed it could no longer compete with Pacific tuna processors in Thailand and American Samoa.[97]

Although the impossibility to sell dolphin-unsafe tuna in the US after the move of the big canneries and the related embargo on Mexico was not the only reason for the economic problems of the small canneries, it is obvious that this policy aggravated their economic decline.

5.4 THE TUNA FISHERMEN – A DECLINING INTEREST GROUP

Traditionally, most of the US tuna fishing fleet was located in California and used to harvest in the ETP. Their strength as an interest group in the political process crucially depended on two factors: firstly, the group size, especially in terms of employment and, secondly, the fishermen's long-standing alliance with the tuna canneries.

The size of the US tuna fishing fleet, and, hence, their employment peaked in the 1980s.[98] Section 5.4.1 analyses the decrease in the fleet size after the tuna price depression which started at the beginning of the 1980s.

Furthermore, section 5.4.2 deals with the relocation of parts of the US tuna fleet which weakened the interest group, especially with respect to the tuna–dolphin issue. Those seamen who permanently left the ETP lost interest in the dolphin protection laws because the close relationship between tunas and dolphins and, hence, the incidental killing of dolphins during the tuna harvest only existed in the ETP.

5.4.1 The Shrinking Fleet

The US tuna canning industry in California can be traced back to the beginning of the century. In the 1930s, with efficient refrigeration available, these vessels mainly harvested in US waters and off the Mexican, central American and South American coast. In the 1950s and the beginning of the 1960s, the bulk of the US fleet still consisted of baitboats.[99]

Table 5.7 The US tuna purse seine fleet: fleet size, additions, removals, 1 January 1978 to 1 January 1992

Year	Fleet size on 1 January		Additions during year		Removals during year		Net change during year	
	No.	Capac- ity[a]	No.	Capac- ity[a]	No.	Capac- ity[a]	No.	Capac- ity[a]
1978	124	110,665	4	4,800	6	6,356	−2	−1,556
1979	122	109,109	5	6,600	3	2,120	2	4,480
1980	124	113,589	5	6,000	12	12,240	−7	−6,240
1981	117	107,349	13	14,750	2	905	11	13,845
1982	128	121,194	11	13,250	14	10,271	−3	2,979
1983	125	124,173	6	7,750	7	5,759	−1	1,991
1984	124	126,164	0	0	17	15,179	−17	−15,179
1985	107	110,985	0	0	17	13,854	−17	−13,854
1986	90	97,131	1	1,500	11	10,742	−10	−9,242
1987	80	87,889	4	3,800	13	13,510	−9	−9,710
1988	71	78,179	3	4,400	11	12,650	−8	−8,250
1989	63	69,929	3	3,700	3	2,670	0	−1,030
1990	63	72,370	3	4,350	10	9,580	−7	−5,230
1991	56	67,140	2	2,850	1	1,100	1	1,750
1992[b]	57	68,890	0	0	4	3,550	−4	−3,550

Source: compiled from data published by US International Trade Commission (1986, p. 158) and US International Trade Commission (1992, p. D3).

Notes:
[a] Capacity in short tons, carrying capacity.
[b] As of January 1992 there were three inactive vessels totalling 3,100 tons.

In the 1960s, the US tuna fishing fleet underwent a serious change triggered by the new technology of purse seiners. Within just ten years, 90 per cent of the US tuna fleet was replaced by purse seiners.[100] In the ETP, the only waters where the special form of tuna dolphin coexistence can be observed, this new harvesting technique introduced the problem of the incidental killing of dolphins.

The US fleet size had steadily increased in the ETP until 1979/1980. At that time, the tuna prices were severely depressed and, according to the US International Trade Commission,[101] the US purse seiners incurred severe losses. The decreasing fleet size is shown in table 5.7 to 5.9.

Table 5.8 The US tuna purse seine fleet: summary of removals by type,
1 January 1978 to 1 January 1992

Year	Lost at sea		Transfer to other fishery		Transfer to foreign flag		Total removals	
	No.	Capac-ity^a	No.	Capac-ity^a	No.	Capac-ity^a	No.	Capac-ity^a
1978	2	2,295	0	0	4	4,061	6	6,356
1979	2	1,570	0	0	1	550	3	2,120
1980	2	1,440	1	300	9	10,500	12	12,240
1981	1	355	0	0	1	550	2	905
1982	6	2,581	0	0	8	7,690	14	10,271
1983	2	678	0	0	5	5,081	7	5,759
1984	4	3,605	2	2,200	11	9,374	17	15,179
1985	2	438	6	4,831	9	8,585	17	13,854
1986	3	2,242	1	950	7	7,750	11	10,942
1987	1	1,400	0	0	12	12,110	13	13,510
1988	0	0	0	0	11	12,650	11	12,650
1989	1	270	0	0	2	2,400	3	2,670
1990	1	1,200	0	0	9	8,380	10	9,580
1991^b	1	1,100	0	0	0	0	1	1,100

Source: compiled from data provided by US International Trade Commission (1986, p. 158) and US International Trade Commission (1992, p. D3).

Notes:
^{a} Capacity in short tons, carrying capacity.
^{b} As of January 1992 there were three inactive vessels totalling 3,100 tons.

As a consequence, the total employment in the tuna purse seiner fleet decreased. From 1980 to 1991 there were 84 vessels with a capacity of almost 85,000 short tons sold abroad. Sailing under a foreign flag, non-US crews were hired in order to decrease the costs of labour. Furthermore, those purse seiners joining the US fleet were significantly larger and used more labour-saving technologies than their predecessors. Therefore, the average number of seamen needed to operate a fishing vessel with the same capacity decreased.

However, the decrease in employment in the US fleet was much larger than the decrease in the harvesting capacity. Furthermore, foreign flag vessels could directly supply the van Camp and the StarKist cannery on American Samoa. In addition, the canneries owned by Asian parent companies imported an increasing number of tuna loins for their US plants, thereby circumventing the high US customs duties for canned tuna in oil.

Since tuna was abundant in the world market and a lot of their own purse seiners had incurred losses, the US canneries started to divest in the harvesting sector.[102] This also meant that the long-standing strategic alliance with the tuna fleet became unimportant for the big tuna processing companies with the single exception of the embargo against tuna from Mexico.

Table 5.9 The US tuna purse seine fleet: summary of additions by type,
*   1 January 1978 to 1 January 1992*

Year	New		Transfer from other fishery		Total additions	
	No.	Capacity[a]	No.	Capacity[a]	No.	Capacity[a]
1978	4	4 800	0	0	4	4,800
1979	5	6 600	0	0	5	6,600
1980	5	6,000	0	0	5	6,000
1981	5	6,000	8	8,750	13	14,750
1982	6	7,200	5	6,050	11	13,250
1983	4	4,950	2	2,800	6	7,750
1984	0	0	0	0	0	0
1985	0	0	0	0	0	0
1986	1	1,500	0	0	1	1,500
1987	1	1,200	3	2,600	4	3,800
1988	1	1,200	2	3,200	3	4,400
1989	1	1,500	2	2,200	3	3,700
1990	3	4,350	0	0	3	4,350
1991[b]	2	2,850	0	0	2	2,850

Source: compiled from data provided by US International Trade Commission (1986, p. 158), and US International Trade Commission (1992, p. D3).

Notes:
[a] Capacity in short tons, carrying capacity.
[b] As of January 1992 there were three inactive vessels totalling 3,100 tons.

5.4.2 Shifts in the US Tuna Fleet Location

In the 1980s, a big part of the US tuna purse seiners shifted from the ETP to the WTP. Some of the reasons were related to the natural resource itself. Additional pressure came from restricted access for US vessels to the tuna fishing grounds after the introduction of 200 mile Economic exclusive zones.

Resource-related factors

Table 5.10 illustrates the declining presence of US tuna purse seiners in the ETP. An increase of the size of the tuna fishing fleet in the ETP led to problems of overusing the resource. By 1966, restrictions were already put on the harvest of yellowfin tuna in the ETP. Despite all efforts there was – starting in 1972 – a serious decline in the so-called catch per standard day's fishing.[103] It reached its lowest levels in the same year as the member countries of the Inter-American Tropical Tuna Commission could not agree on how to implement a new conservation programme in 1979/1980.[104] Due to the shortage of yellowfin tuna, some purse seiners started to shift to the WTP.

Table 5.10 Number and capacity of US purse seiners in the ETP, 1980–92

Year	Number of purse seiners	Total capacity/ short tons	Year	Number of purse seiners	Total capacity/ short tons
1980	126	105,022	1987	54	41,965
1981	128	107,272	1988	60	44,568
1982	123	104,120	1989	51	33,009
1983	100	77,532	1990	28	27,120
1984	73	46,248	1991	17	16,590
1985	67	45,113	1992	9	8,990
1986	64	43,235			

Source: data compiled from various Annual Reports of the Inter-American Tropical Tuna Commission.

An El-Niño started in the Pacific Ocean in 1982. It peaked in 1983 and subsided in late 1983. This phenomenon is a warm water event which heavily affects the tuna catch. Although El-Niños have occurred previously,[105] the event of 1982/83 was considered to be the strongest since the beginning of century. In 1982, the yellowfin catch was 52 per cent and the skipjack catch just reached 40 per cent of the average catch for the 1977–81 period. 'During 1982 and 1983 many large seiners sailed to the western Pacific, where the vessels, which were already there, were making good catches.'[106] Although it was found that the yellowfin resources had recovered when the El-Niño subsided, a lot of purse seiners had to stay in the WTP since the canneries had in the meantime shifted most of their capacities to American Samoa as shown in figure 5.2. 'The resulting increased transportation costs, during a time of rising harvesting costs and declining prices, contributed to the decisions of many US vessel operators to either move their operations to the western Pacific or cease active participation in the US tuna fishery altogether.'[107]

metric tons

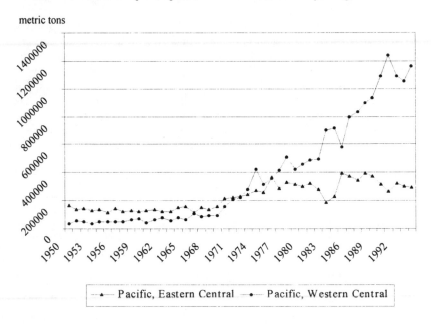

Source: FAO (1994): *Fishery Statistics – Catches and Landings.*

Figure 5.2 Tuna catches in ETP and WTP, 1950–92

Hence, the El-Niño phenomenon, along with the problems of the yellowfin conservation in the ETP, contributed to the fishermen's relocation decision. The group of fishermen, therefore, which had an interest to actively resist the strengthening of the 'dolphin-safe' laws in the Eastern Tropical Pacific further declined because the tuna–dolphin problem does not exist in the WTP.

Political problems leading to relocation
The question of access to tuna resources became more pressing for the US tuna fleet in the 1970s and also contributed to their relocation. When the US vessels started to fish off the coast of most Central and South American countries in the 1950s, 3–12 mile Economic exclusive zone did not constitute a major obstacle. In the 1970s, most the Central American countries began to

extend their EEZ to 200 miles.[108] However, the US did not recognise EEZ prior to 1977 and even afterwards, they did not accept other countries' jurisdiction over tuna outside the 12-mile zone. The US argument was that tunas 'are highly migratory, and that no nation effectively has the ability to manage tuna resources'.[109] By this arrangement the US did not lose economically because they gave other countries' tuna vessels free access to their waters where hardly any tuna is abundant. Otherwise, 70 per cent of the ETP tuna can be found in the Mexican EEZ. The access problem, from the United States point of view, became more serious when Mexico, Ecuador and Costa Rica withdrew from the Inter-American Tropical Tuna Commission. A common management of the depleted yellowfin tuna stocks was no longer possible.[110] Negotiations to ensure access to the tuna resources of the ETP for the US tuna vessels basically failed over a disagreement about the tuna quota to be allocated to the Central and South American countries.[111] After seizures of US vessels in the Mexican EEZ, an embargo on the country's tuna products started in 1986.[112] This benefited the US tuna canneries insofar as the development of the Mexican tuna industry was constrained without access to the US market. Otherwise, the US purse seiner fleet suffered from limited access to the ETP-resources although US vessels were insured against seizures under the MFCMA. Baitboat and longliner owners negotiated a separate access agreement. The Mexican government, however, did not renew the agreement because of the embargo imposed by the MMPA in 1990. Once again, the breakdown of the strategic alliance between the tuna canneries and the tuna fishermen in the ETP weakened their position and contributed to the relocation of the fleet to the WTP.

Although the problem of access to the EEZ existed in the WTP as well, the ability of the island nations to enforce their EEZ was very limited. This imposed minimal risk on US vessels fishing in these grounds and, increasingly, the tuna industry negotiated individual access agreements. Furthermore, in 1986, the US government completed a treaty with the South Pacific Fisheries Agency (SPFA), which has granted licensed access to its waters to up to 50 US fishing vessels.[113] In turn, the US accepted the SPFA's jurisdiction within the EEZ. Hence, the supply of tuna for the US canneries on American Samoa has always been ensured. Finally, in 1992, the US generally recognised the countries' jurisdiction over tuna in the EEZ, which also ended the insurance of US vessels against seizures.

The difficulties of obtaining access to the tuna fishing grounds in the ETP in the mid 1980s contributed to the relocation of the US purse seiner fleet to the WTP. The number of fishermen remaining on purse seiners in the ETP decreased even further due to technological improvements on the ships. Therefore, the number of those seafarers with a personal interest in resisting a further tightening of the dolphin-safe standard became smaller. In the 1980s it became obvious that the tuna fishermen could only secure their interests with respect to the tuna–dolphin issue without an alliance with the US tuna canneries. Such an alliance was possible in the case of the WTP access agreements because that was vital for the fishing fleet and the plants on American Samoa. With respect to the ETP, such treaties could not be negotiated. The position of the US purse seiner crews further deteriorated by the implementation of the dolphin-safe policy and the recognition of the EEZ by the US in 1992, which left the vessels still fishing in the ETP without insurance against seizure.

5.5 THE ENVIRONMENTALISTS

The environmentalists are probably the group which most obviously belongs to the winning coalition in the struggle over the re-authorisation of the MMPA in 1988 and the implementation of the International Dolphin Protection Consumer Information Act. Although the coalition of environmentalists[114] seemed to be quite homogenous in their interest in protecting the dolphins, the disagreement over the Panama declaration of 1995,[115] which was meant to pave the way for the US tuna embargo, revealed rather different approaches to the protection of dolphins among the different groups.

The environmentalists basically consist of two subgroups. On the one hand, there are interest groups which have multidimensional goals with respect to the protection of the environment, such as the World Wide Fund for Nature (WWF) or Greenpeace. On the other hand, there are groups which are primarily interested in the protection of marine mammals in general, and dolphins in particular.

The Earth Island Institute (EII) which spearheaded the 1988/1990 campaign for tightening the MMPA and the introduction of the Dolphin Protection Consumer Information Act belonged – among others – to the second group mentioned above. Until the mid 1990s, both subgroups were basically of the same opinion with respect to the necessity of measures to protect dolphins.

In 1988, the discussion concerning the re-authorisation of the MMPA was galvanised by Sam LaBudde who – on behalf of the Earth Island Institute – showed a video on the killing of 50 dolphins during a single harvesting operation. He filmed pictures during the fishing trip of a Panamanian vessel.[116] The industry was harshly attacked for behaving in deviance to their policy statements with respect to the protection of dolphins.

Although the film turned out to be very influential in the public discussion and was prominently broadcasted in the ABC-News, the tuna canneries hardly made use of the fact that the Inter-American Tropical Tuna Commission found out just a few weeks later that the Panamanian vessel was in no respect representative for the tuna harvest in the ETP.[117] At the same time, reports in US newspapers pointed out that US observers on tuna purse seiners were forced by the crew to report wrong numbers of killed dolphins. However, while the campaign of the environmentalist pressure groups appeared to be extremely well organised, the reaction of the US tuna industry was very defensive.[118] They only pointed out that the vessel was not a US vessel.[119]

This supports the hypothesis that the success of the powerful 1988/1990 campaign of the environmentalist groups was also due to the industries' lacking will to resist stricter laws.

5.6 RECENT DEVELOPMENTS IN THE US DOLPHIN-SAFE POLICY

Another attempt to strengthen the dolphin-safe standards was launched in 1992.[120] The International Dolphin Conservation Act of 1992 proposed a moratorium on catching tuna in the ETP with purse seine nets. The law required that before the moratorium could go into effect at least one country with a purse seiner fleet in the ETP had to enter into an agreement with the US prior to 1 January 1994 prohibiting fishing on dolphins. No other country joined the US initiative and the agreement never came into force.

In April 1992, the member countries of the IATTC[121] agreed on the La Jolla declaration with the goal of '(1) progressively reducing dolphin mortality in the EPO fishery to levels approaching zero through the setting of annual limits and (2) with a goal of eliminating dolphin mortality in this fishery . . . while maintaining the population of yellowfin tuna in the EPO at a level which will permit maximum sustained catches year after year . . . '[122] The IATTC-countries signed the Declaration of Panama in 1995.[123] It modified some provisions of the La Jolla Agreement and the nations committed themselves 'to an approach aimed at the conservation of the ecosystem to which the tunas and dolphins belong rather than only one or two of its components.'[124] Some environmentalist groups such as the Center for Marine Conservation, the Environmental Defense Fund, Greenpeace, the National Wildlife Federation and the World Wide Fund for Nature, signed a joint statement of support for the declaration because they were increasingly worried about the by-catch problem[125] caused by dolphin-safe tuna harvest. The Panama Declaration and the La Jolla Agreement required all countries to bring their national dolphin protection programmes in line with the agreement, and obliged the US to lift the tuna embargoes on Mexico and other countries. Bills aimed at this were introduced in the US Congress.[126] The House passed the legislation with 306 to 108 in a roll call vote on 31 July 1996. However, the Senate could not pass the bill, partly because Senator Barbara Boxer who put forward the 1990 legislation, threatened filibustering.[127] In July 1997 the new legislation finally passed Congress after the supporters found a compromise with those 44 senators who blocked the measure from coming to a floor vote. The bill allows tuna to carry the label 'dolphin-safe' if an independent observer certifies that in the particular catch no dolphin was killed. However, the new rules will only come into force if an 18-month long government study shows that dolphins released from the nets after encirclement do not suffer from trauma which prevent them, for example, from reproduction.[128] The new policy was mainly driven by three forces.

5.6.1 External pressure

The US environmental legislation, especially the embargo provisions of the MMPA, were found to be inconsistent with the obligations of the United States under the GATT twice.[129] During the negotiations on NAFTA and the completion of the Uruguay Round, neither Mexico asked for the implementation of the first panel decision nor did the European Union ask for the adoption of the second ruling.[130] However, there was great pressure on the US to bring their environmental legislation in line with the requirements of the GATT. Mexico, in particular, has refused to put too much pressure on the US thus far in order to give the US government time to push for a change in regulation without accusations being made that American laws are imposed by international organisations outside the US or foreign countries. After most countries, which are parties to the Declaration of Panama, implemented the required stricter dolphin protection standards, the US was obliged to lift the embargo on Mexico.

5.6.2 Split in the Environmental Community

Some environmentalist groups have been increasingly worried about the by-catch problem that arises from dolphin-safe tuna fishing. Only mature tuna are associated with dolphins and the strict dolphin-safe standards encourage the fishermen to set on immature tunas which would have an negative effect on the population. Furthermore, the by-catch, which is higher, setting on dolphin-safe tuna, consists of a lot of other species such as billfish, sharks, mahi-mahi and some sea-turtles,[131] some of which are endangered. Some environmentalists support the Panama declaration, whereas others violently oppose the change in the dolphin-safe definition. One possible dividing line between these groups is whether they are purely concerned with dolphin protection or whether they have a multidimensional approach to the protection of the marine environment. However, the split among the environmentalists weakened the coalition in favour of maintaining the dolphin-safe definition of the Boxer Bill.

5.6.3 Newly Emerging Interest Groups

The local fishing fleets in California, currently consisting mainly of baitboats and longliners, have always supported measures to lift the embargo on Mexican tuna in order to be able to negotiate an access agreement for the Mexican EEZ. This group is now supported by newly emerging sushi and sashimi restaurants, for whom it is essential to gain access to fresh tuna, which can only be harvested in the ETP. Although not really important in the political process thus far, this group joined the large coalition of supporters of the new dolphin-safe definition.

5.7 CONCLUSIONS

This chapter examined the different pressure groups' interest in the US dolphin-safe legislation from 1989 to 1991. In these years, Congress gave up a policy of balancing the interests of tuna fishing and dolphin protection in the ETP in favour of more protection of the marine mammals.

In explaining this policy reversal, the analysis does not deny the growing importance of Green interest groups in the political process. But a closer investigation of the different US pressure groups' goals made clear that the canneries and the fishermen had no reason to actively resist the new regulation. This result is contrary to the public perception because both groups' economic interest in tuna fishing in the ETP had changed prior to 1989 without much public attention.

The tuna fishing fleet left the ETP for the most part and the tuna harvest in other regions was not affected by the new standards. Hence, only a few US fishermen were really affected by the dolphin protection standards while the others were indifferent to the decision. The canneries had lost their previously high interest in the region after they had relocated almost all of their factories to other regions in the 1980s. Furthermore, support for tighter dolphin protection standards and the sudden policy change in 1990 opened up rent-seeking opportunities. Their small domestic rivals were forced out of the market. More importantly, Mexico, as a potentially strong competitor in the market for canned tuna, was boycotted.

The results of the study are supported by the discussion prior to the revision of the MMPA in 1997.

NOTES

1   This chapter is based on Körber (1998).
2   The press mainly advocated the hypothesis that the Greens completely defeated the other interest groups. See, for example, Shabecoff (1990), *New York Times* (1990).

3   Bonanno and Constance (1996) use a study on the Tuna–Dolphin Case to prove their
     argument of 'contradictory convergence', which refers to the weakening of the nation state
     through globalisation.
4   See CQ-Almanac (1972, p. 961).
5   In the Western Tropical Pacific, for example, tunas are frequently located by helicopters
     or, less commonly, by observing bird (feeding) activity. See Felando (1988, p. 117).
6   See General Agreement on Tariffs and Trade (1991, p. 2).
7   See Inter-American Tropical Tuna Commission (1984, p. 227).
8   See Colson (1992, p. 15).
9   The Reid-Amendment was refused with a 17–47 standing vote. See CQ-Almanac (1972,
     p. 964).
10   In 1975, the National Marine Fisheries Service (NMFS) issued a dolphin mortality quota
     of 78,000. In 1981 it was reduced to 20,500 where it remained until the end of the 1980s.
     See National Research Council (1992, p. 27).
11   See US Congress (1981).
12   Just in the re-authorisation process of 1977 disagreement about the quota was reported
     when a new upper limit of dolphins which could be killed incidentally was set. In response
     to a court ruling, the NMFS set a quota of 59,050 in that year. After fishermen's
     interventions, the Chairman of the House Merchant Marine and Fisheries Committee
     promised to raise the quota to 78,900. This, in turn, was challenged by environmentalists
     who succeeded in reducing the committee proposal for a quota to 68,910. Before the bill
     could finally be passed, it was reported that fishermen had only taken 21,000 dolphins by
     October. This ended the push for legislation. See CQ-Almanac (1977, p. 674).
13   See US Congress (1988). According to US Public Law PL100-711, the State Department
     had been required since 1984 to report on foreign dolphin conservation measures. It
     regularly found these standards comparable with the US regulation.
14   See US District Court-N.D. California (1990).
15   For details see, for example, General Agreement on Tariffs and Trade (1991) and General
     Agreement on Tariffs and Trade (1994a).
16   See US International Trade Commission (1990, p. 2.5).
17   The value of US canned tuna production rose from US$ 820 million in 1985 to US$ 1.1
     billion in 1989. See US International Trade Commission (1990, p. 2.11).
18   See King (1987, p. 77).
19   See US International Trade Commission (1990, p. 2.16).
20   See American Samoa Government (1994).
21   See H.J. Heinz Company (1985, p. 17).
22   See StarKist (1996, pp. 1–2).
23   See US International Trade Commission (1990, p. 2.16).
24   See Floyd (1987, p. 87).
25   For the impact of loining on the companies' interest in the ETP, see section 5.3.2 and
     section 5.6.
26   See Handley (1991a, p. 50).
27   See section 5.3.2.
28   See Handley (1991a, p. 48).
29   See StarKist (1996, pp. 1–2).
30   See US International Trade Commission (1990, p. 2.17).
31   See US International Trade Commission (1990, p. 2.18).
32   See US International Trade Commission (1986, p. 23).
33   For the decreasing political influence of the tuna fishermen from the ETP, see section 5.4.
34   See Studds (1990, p. 53).
35   See Ramirez (1990, p. D1).
36   O'Reilly (1990, p. 327).
37   See, for example, *New York Times* (1990, p. 22).
38   See Ramirez (1990, p. D1).

39   See Young (1990, p. 55).
40   See US International Trade Commission (1986, p. 28).
41   This applies to the full-fledged canneries. After having developed an efficient loining technology in the late 1980s, a loining factory was opened in Santa Fe, Ca. All other American canneries are either located in Puerto Rico or American Samoa.
42   See *Seafood International* (1988, p. 29).
43   See US International Trade Commission (1992, p. 2.2) and US International Trade Commission (1986, p. 29). It is not possible to obtain total landing data for American Samoa alone. According to the National Marine Fisheries Service, the data are by federal statute confidential when there are less than three dealers or seafood processors on one island.
44   See US International Trade Commission (1990, p. 2.18).
45   The figures were provided by the Economic Development Planning Office of the Government of American Samoa.
46   See US International Trade Commission (1992, p. D23). The International Trade Commission compiled their tables from data submitted in response to its questionnaires.
47   See US International Trade Commission (1990, 2.23–2.24).
48   This section of the Internal Revenue Act is codified in 26 USC s 936.
49   Sec. 936 applies to Guam, American Samoa, and Puerto Rico. It is derived from a provision of the 1922 China Trade Act, the purpose of which was to enable US corporations doing business in China to compete with local British corporations, which enjoyed the same exemption from British taxes. See US International Trade Commission (1990, p. 2.23).
50   See US International Trade Commission (1990, p. 2.22).
51   See American Samoa Government (1994, p. 133).
52   The tariff for canned tuna in oil is even higher; it is 36 per cent. See section 5.3.2.
53   Floyd (1987, p. 85).
54   See US International Trade Commission (1990, p. 2.4).
55   See King (1987, p. 71).
56   See Doulman and Kearney (1987).
57   Tuna catches are measured in metric tons or MT.
58   Compiled from Data of the Food and Agriculture Organization (1994). All catches refer to ISSCAAP Species group 36 'Tunas, bonitos, billfish, etc.', ISSCAAP = International Standard Statistical Classification of Aquatic Animals and Plants.
59   Different fishing conditions make larger nets necessary. In order to handle these nets, upgraded winches and booms had to be adopted. A larger vessel size was developed for the WTP mainly to handle these larger nets, see US International Trade Commission (1992, p. 5.4).
60   See US International Trade Commission (1986, p. 23).
61   See Muñoz (1990, p. 50).
62   See section 5.3.3 for an explanation of why the import quota was gradually decreased by the canneries' locational decisions during the 1980s.
63   See Handley (1989, p. 108).
64   See Burton (1989, p. 108 9).
65   This measure was legislated as public law PL98-364.
66   The measure became public law PL100-711.
67   See Colson (1992, p. 15).
68   These were particularly requirements concerning nets, the backdown procedure, the use of the Medina panel, and the compulsory participation in the observer programme of the Inter-American Tropical Tuna Commission (IATTC). See also section 3.2.
69   Environmentalists led by the California based Earth Island Institute had sued the US Department of Commerce. See US District Court-N.D. California (1990).
70   See General Agreement on Tariffs and Trade (1991) and General Agreement on Tariffs and Trade (1994a).

71 The number of dolphins which could be killed incidentally by the foreign fleets was tied, as already mentioned, to the number of dolphins killed by the US fleet in the ETP.
72 See Colson (1992, p. 15).
73 For an analysis of the fishermen's interests, see section 5.4; for those of the environmentalists see section 5.5.
74 Burney (1988b, p. 132).
75 See US National Marine Fisheries Service (1987).
76 See section 5.3.2.
77 See US International Trade Commission (1990, p. 5.18).
78 See US International Trade Commission (1990, p. 5.19).
79 See Hudgins (1987, p. 157).
80 Other canneries are located in Baja California Sur and Sinaloa.
81 See US International Trade Commission (1990, p. 5.20).
82 See US International Trade Commission (1986, p. 117–8).
83 See US International Trade Commission (1986, pp. 101–105). The MFCMA is concerned with the extension of the US Economic exclusive zone. A brief summary of the issue is given in section 5.4.2.
84 In November 1990, the US finally agreed to include tuna under the jurisdiction of the 200-miles Economic exclusive zone.
85 See Inter-American Tropical Tuna Commission (1981, p. 17).
86 Hudgins (1987, p. 156).
87 See US District Court-N.D. California (1990).
88 For a theoretical discussion, see Salop and Scheffman (1983).
89 See US International Trade Commission (1990, p. 2.13).
90 See US International Trade Commission (1990, p. 2.13).
91 See Mitsubishi Foods (MC) (1990, p. 325–6). As noted earlier, the Earth Island Institute had threatened the tuna canneries with a consumer boycott should they proceed in selling dolphin-unsafe tuna.
92 See US International Trade Commission (1992, p. 5.9).
93 See US International Trade Commission (1992, p. 5.9–5.10).
94 See US International Trade Commission (1992, p. 4.2).
95 Thus, the dolphin-safe issue which was the justification of the tuna embargo prevented a successful negotiation with Mexico on access to its fishing grounds.
96 See *Los Angeles Times* (1995). Later Pan Pacific was bought out of bankruptcy by Tri-Marine, which is the world's largest trading company in tuna and related products. The company claimed that it wanted to utilise the local fishing fleet's catch and to shift production from sole tuna canning to include the processing of mackerels, sardines and squid. See also section 5.6.
97 See Associated Press (1995).
98 The fleet of tuna purse seiners reached their highest number in 1982 and the highest capacity in 1984. See tables 5.7–5.9.
99 See US International Trade Commission (1986, pp. 7–8).
100 See US International Trade Commission (1986, p. 7).
101 See US International Trade Commission (1992, p. D8).
102 The US canneries had been vertically integrated with the purse seiner fleet since the introduction of this technique in the 1960s. At the beginning of the 1980s the canneries had divested completely in the harvesting sector. See section 5.3.2 and US International Trade Commission (1986, p. 17).
103 See Inter-American Tropical Tuna Commission (1993, p. 207).
104 See Inter-American Tropical Tuna Commission (1985, p. 23).
105 El-Niños also occurred in 1957–58 and 1972–73. Inter-American Tropical Tuna Commission (1985, p. 69). In 1997–98 there was another El Niño which was considered to be comparable to the 1982/83 event. See US National Oceanic and Atmospheric Administration (1997).

106 Inter-American Tropical Tuna Commission (1984, p. 69).
107 US International Trade Commission (1986, p. 11).
108 Dates of extension to a 200 mile economic exclusion zone: Chile (1947), Peru (1947), El Salvador (1950), Ecuador (1951), Colombia (1978), Nicaragua (1965), Panama (1967), Costa Rica (1975), Guatemala (1976), Mexico (1976), Honduras (1980). See US International Trade Commission (1986, p. 102).
109 See US International Trade Commission (1990, p. 1.3).
110 See section 5.4.2.
111 See US International Trade Commission (1986, p. 103).
112 See section 5.3.3. The legal basis for the embargo was the Magnuson Act.
113 See US International Trade Commission (1990, pp. 4.3–4.4).
114 Among others, this coalition consisted of Animal Protection Institute of America, California Marine Mammal Center, Defenders of Wildlife, Earth Island Institute, Friends of the Earth, Greenpeace, Marine Mammal Fund, Oceanic Society, Society for Animal Protective Legislation, The Humane Society of the United States, etc. See Scheele (1988, p. 105).
115 See Declaration of Panama (1995) and section 5.6.
116 See LaBudde (1988).
117 See Joseph (1988).
118 It is often said that in the beginning of the dolphin campaign, the EEI was financially supported by the US canneries. However, EEI did not respond to inquiries in order to validate this information.
119 See Burney (1988a, pp. 135–6).
120 See Joseph (1996, pp. 330–1).
121 Observers from NGOs also were present, notably from the Animal Protection Institute of America, the Center for Marine Conservation, the Earth Island Institute, Greenpeace, etc.
122 For the La Jolla Agreement, see Inter-American Tropical Tuna Commission (1993, pp. 8–10).
123 See Declaration of Panama (1995).
124 Joseph (1996, p. 333).
125 The dolphin-safe tuna harvest turned out to be dangerous for sharks, sea turtles, and other animals some of which are endangered species. See section 6.2.
126 In the House introduced as H.R. 2823, International Dolphin Conservation Program Act by Rep. Gilchrest, and in the Senate introduced as S. 1420 by Sen. Stevens.
127 See *Japan Times* (1996), p.22. The bill, H.R. 408 and S. 39 were sponsored by Rep. Gilchrest in the House and Sen. Stevens in the Senate.
128 H.R. 408/S.39 became Public Law No. 105–42 on 15 August 1997.
129 For a detailed discussion, see section 2.4.3.
130 See Goldberg (1994a), Goldberg (1994b).
131 See Joseph (1996).

6. Concluding Remarks

The terms 'Trade and Environment' describe a bundle of different aspects regarding the interrelationship between international trade and protection of the environment. From the point of view of 'free traders', the abuse of environmental regulation turns out to be one of the most worrying features. Again, it must be emphasised that there is no general concern about environmental regulation. However, the high desirability of a clean environment should not prevent a thorough analysis of the potential side effects of environmental regulation on trade. Furthermore, not every claim that a certain measure is used to protect the environment should be taken at its face value. A leitmotiv of this study was that different interest groups can side with each other to push for the same kind of environmental regulation interests for completely different reasons.

The study aimed at explaining the abuse of environmental regulation. Thus, the analysis had to answer three interrelated questions. First, *why* do we observe so much protectionism although the superiority of free trade is one of economists most cherished beliefs? Second, *what* makes environmental legislation a particularly desirable instrument of trade protection and *how* do these features fit in with the models explaining trade protection? Third, what is the practical relevance of environmental protectionism?

The answer to the first question required a thorough analysis of those arguments justifying a deviation from free trade. The deficiencies of the models using a first- or a second-best framework with the unrealistic assumptions of a benevolent dictator paved the way for the use of the political economic approach to trade protection. The incorporation of gainers and losers from free trade into the models yields a convincing explanation for the extent of the observed trade protection.

The answer to the first part of the second question required an investigation of the institutional details of the world trading system. It showed that the trade rules leave room for the *legal* application of trade-distorting measures. The analysis of the main exception clause of the WTO Treaty, Art. XX, and several panel rulings showed that there is potential for a country to escape its obligations under the treaty. The argument is not flawed by the fact that most panel rulings so far reject claims for the use of the escape clause. First, only those cases which are controversial are brought to the panel.

Second, disputes, such as the Thai Cigarette Case,[1] were very blunt attempts at protectionism and the fact that the GATT requires more than 'just mentioning' of the term environment is not a real barrier to qualify for Art. XX. However, purely national environmental regulation which results in discriminatory treatment of domestic and foreign industries has even more potential as a protectionist measure. The auto panel decision[2] made it clear that effective discrimination is not equivalent to the legal term 'discriminatory' used by the GATT. Furthermore, the success of the trade negotiations in the framework of the GATT or WTO, especially the Uruguay Round, restricted the use of other protectionist instruments. The incorporation of the Tokyo Round Codes into the WTO Agreement, the prohibition of VERs, and restrictions on the use of anti-dumping made a lot of new non-tariff barriers unavailable to governments. This has already caused a 'substitution effect' towards the use of environmental regulation.

Additionally, and most importantly, the political process of environmental decision making contains features which are very attractive for protectionist interests. First, pushing for environmental regulation makes it easier for protectionist interests to obfuscate the true intent of the political activity. Additionally, the 'irreversibility' of environmental regulation and the existence of potentially powerful allies for the protectionist interest increases the probability of implementing environmental regulation.

The use of lobbying models, however, makes a closer look at the political process necessary. The contest–success function is at the centre of economic models of lobbying. For a fairly general function, the conditions for a two-sided or one-sided lobbying contest turned out to be restrictive. The models introduced in Chapter 4 specifically aimed at formalising the idea of raising rivals' costs. Both versions, the total exclusion of the foreign firm from the market and less drastic increase of the foreign firm's costs compared to its domestic competitor, were considered. The 'irreversibility' led to decreasing expected gains and expected losses from environmental regulation over time for firm 1 and firm 2, respectively. This feature triggered changed lobbying strategies of the firms at different stages of the game. Additionally, the introduction of a more realistic (two-staged) decision process, made it clear that the Greens' lobbying activities can increase the probability of environmental regulation despite the public good properties of the contested price in Nash equilibria.

A detailed case study showed that there is evidence that in the tuna–dolphin cases, ecological protectionism and raising rivals' costs played an important role. Analysing the actors' economic interests, which changed over time, led to the conclusion that – to say the least – the choice of the environmental policy instrument benefited the most powerful interest group significantly. The case study, which centres around a ban on tuna imports from Mexico, which has lasted for more than seven years, showed that environmental regulation can lead to massive trade distortions and a significant change in the domestic competition situation. This book particularly stressed that even environmental regulation, which is successful in terms of an improvement in the environmental conditions, can incorporate highly trade-distorting elements and that some groups might push for this regulation, particularly because of these elements.

NOTES

1   See General Agreement on Tariffs and Trade (1990).
2   See General Agreement on Tariffs and Trade (1994b).

Appendices

1. THE DICHOTOMOUS MODEL OF RAISING RIVALS' COSTS

Table A1   The dichotomous model – payoffs in period 2

Outcome	U_H	U_F
1	π^M	0
2	$\pi^M - L_H$	$-L_F$
3	$\pi^D - L_H$	$\pi^D - L_F$
4	$\pi^M - L_H$	0
5	$\pi^D - L_H$	π^D
6	π^D	$\pi^D - L_F$
7	π^D	π^D
8	π^M	0
9	$\pi^M - L_H$	$-L_F$
10	$\pi^D - L_H$	$\pi^D - L_F$
11	$\pi^M - L_H$	0
12	$\pi^D - L_H$	π^D
13	π^D	$\pi^D - L_F$
14	π^D	π^D
15	$\pi^M - L_H$	$-L_F$
16	$\pi^D - L_H$	$\pi^D - L_F$
17	$\pi^M - L_H$	0
18	$\pi^D - L_H$	π^D
19	π^D	$\pi^D - L_F$
20	π^D	π^D
21	$\pi^M - L_H$	$-L_F$
22	$\pi^D - L_H$	$\pi^D - L_F$
23	$\pi^M - L_H$	0
24	$\pi^D - L_H$	π^D
25	π^D	$\pi^D - L_F$
26	π^D	π^D

2. THE DICHOTOMOUS MODEL OF RAISING RIVALS' COSTS – PURE STRATEGY EQUILIBRIA IN THE STATIC CASE (PERIOD 2)

The Firms' Reaction Equations

U_F
Assume $L_H = 1$

$$L_F = \begin{Bmatrix} 1 \\ 0 \end{Bmatrix} \Leftrightarrow (p_2 - p_1)\, \pi^D \begin{Bmatrix} \geq \\ < \end{Bmatrix} 1 \qquad \begin{array}{l}(4.1')\\(4.1'')\end{array}$$

Assume $L_H = 0$

$$L_F = \begin{Bmatrix} 1 \\ 0 \end{Bmatrix} \Leftrightarrow \pi^D - 1 \begin{Bmatrix} \geq \\ < \end{Bmatrix} \pi^D \qquad \begin{array}{l}(4.2')\\(4.2'')\end{array}$$

U_H
Assume $L_F = 1$

$$L_H = \begin{Bmatrix} 1 \\ 0 \end{Bmatrix} \Leftrightarrow p_1\, (\pi^M - \pi^D) \begin{Bmatrix} \geq \\ < \end{Bmatrix} 1 \qquad \begin{array}{l}(4.3')\\(4.3'')\end{array}$$

Assume $L_F = 0$

$$L_H = \begin{Bmatrix} 1 \\ 0 \end{Bmatrix} \Leftrightarrow p_2\, (\pi^M - \pi^D) \begin{Bmatrix} \geq \\ < \end{Bmatrix} 1 \qquad \begin{array}{l}(4.4')\\(4.4'')\end{array}$$

Subgame Equilibria in Period 2

Whether the firms' strategies depicted by the preceding 'reaction equations' are consistent with each other is analysed in this part of the appendix.

$(0, 0)$

$$\pi^D - 1 < \pi^D \qquad (4.2'')$$

$$\wedge \; p_2\, (\pi^M - \pi^D) < 1 \qquad (4.4'')$$

Both conditions can be met at the same time.

(0, 1)

$$\pi^D - 1 \geq \pi^D \qquad (4.2')$$

$$\wedge \; p_1 \, (\pi^M - \pi^D) < 1 \qquad (4.3'')$$

This is not a possible outcome because 4.2' can never be fulfilled simultaneously.

(1, 0)

$$(p_2 - p_1) \, \pi^D < 1 \qquad (4.1'')$$

$$\wedge \; p_2 \, (\pi^M - \pi^D) \geq 1 \qquad (4.4')$$

Both conditions can be fulfilled simultaneously. Substituting 4.1'' with 4.4' leads to $\pi^D \, (2 - p_1/p_2) < \pi^M$ which is always valid because $\pi^M > 2 \, \pi^D$.

(1, 1)

$$(p_2 - p_1) \, \pi^D \geq 1 \qquad (4.1')$$

$$\wedge \; p_1 \, (\pi^M - \pi^D) \geq 1 \qquad (4.3')$$

Solving 4.1' and 4.3' for p_1 yields

$$p_2 \geq \frac{\pi^M}{\left(\pi^M - \pi^D\right) \; \pi^D} .$$

p_1 and p_2 are probabilities and hence the existence of $p_1 < 1 \wedge p_2 \leq 1$ requires $\pi^M/\pi^D \leq \pi^M - \pi^D$.

3. THE DICHOTOMOUS MODEL OF RAISING RIVALS' COSTS – PURE STRATEGY EQUILIBRIA IN PERIOD 1

Subgame Equilibria in Period 1

This appendix is divided into three subsections dealing with the three pure strategy subgame equilibria of period 2. Within these sections, the firms' 'reaction equations' for period 1 are calculated. Afterwards, the firms' strategies are checked for whether or not they are consistent with each other. This leads to the pure-strategy equilibria of period 1 given each pure strategy equilibrium of period 2.

Subgame Equilibrium in Period 2: (0, 0)

The firms' reaction equations

U_F

Assume $L_H = 1$

$$L_F = \begin{Bmatrix} 1 \\ 0 \end{Bmatrix} \Leftrightarrow 2\,(p_2 - p_1)\,\pi^D \begin{Bmatrix} \geq \\ < \end{Bmatrix} 1 \qquad \begin{array}{l} (4.5') \\ (4.5'') \end{array}$$

Assume $L_H = 0$

$$L_F = \begin{Bmatrix} 1 \\ 0 \end{Bmatrix} \Leftrightarrow 2\,\pi^D - 1 \begin{Bmatrix} \geq \\ < \end{Bmatrix} 2\,\pi^D \qquad \begin{array}{l} (4.6') \\ (4.6'') \end{array}$$

U_H

Assume $L_F = 1$

$$L_H = \begin{Bmatrix} 1 \\ 0 \end{Bmatrix} \Leftrightarrow 2\,p_1\,(\pi^M - \pi^D) \begin{Bmatrix} \geq \\ < \end{Bmatrix} 1 \qquad \begin{array}{l} (4.7') \\ (4.7'') \end{array}$$

Assume $L_F = 0$

$$L_H = \begin{Bmatrix} 1 \\ 0 \end{Bmatrix} \Leftrightarrow 2\,p_2\,(\pi^M - \pi^D) \begin{Bmatrix} \geq \\ < \end{Bmatrix} 1 \qquad \begin{array}{l} (4.8') \\ (4.8'') \end{array}$$

Subgame equilibria in period 1

(0, 0)

$$2\,\pi^D - 1 < 2\,\pi^D \qquad (4.6'')$$

$$\wedge\ 2\,p_2\,(\pi^M - \pi^D) < 1 \qquad (4.8'')$$

Both conditions can be fulfilled simultaneously.

(0, 1)

$$2\,\pi^D - 1 \geq 2\,\pi^D \tag{4.6'}$$

$$\wedge\ 2\,p_1\,(\pi^M - \pi^D) < 1 \tag{4.7''}$$

This is not a possible outcome because equation 4.6' can never be fulfilled.

(1, 0)

$$2\,(p_2 - p_1)\,\pi^D < 1 \tag{4.5''}$$

$$\wedge\ 2\,p_2\,(\pi^M - \pi^D) \geq 1 \tag{4.8'}$$

Both conditions can be fulfilled simultaneously.

(1, 1)

$$2\,(p_2 - p_1)\,\pi^D \geq 1 \tag{4.5''}$$

$$2\,p_1\,(\pi^M - \pi^D) \geq 1 \tag{4.7'}$$

If one takes into account equation 4.4' from period 2 all three equations cannot be fulfilled simultaneously.

   If $2\,\pi^D < \pi^M \leq 3\,\pi^D$ (see equations 4.1'' and 4.4''), parameter constellations with no equilibrium in period 1 will exist.

Subgame Equilibrium in Period 2: (1, 0)

The firms' reaction equations

U_F
Assume $L_H = 1$

$$L_F = \begin{Bmatrix} 1 \\ 0 \end{Bmatrix} \Leftrightarrow (2 - p_2)\,(p_2 - p_1)\,\pi^D \begin{Bmatrix} \geq \\ < \end{Bmatrix} 1 \qquad \begin{array}{l} (4.9') \\ (4.9'') \end{array}$$

Assume $L_H = 0$

$$L_F = \begin{Bmatrix} 1 \\ 0 \end{Bmatrix} \Leftrightarrow \pi^D\,(2 - p_2) - 1 \begin{Bmatrix} \geq \\ < \end{Bmatrix} \pi^D\,(2 - p_2) \qquad \begin{array}{l} (4.10') \\ (4.10'') \end{array}$$

U_H
Assume $L_F = 1$

$$L_H = \begin{Bmatrix} 1 \\ 0 \end{Bmatrix} \Leftrightarrow (\pi^M - \pi^D)\, p_1\, (2 - p_2) + p_2 \begin{Bmatrix} \geq \\ < \end{Bmatrix} 1 \qquad \begin{matrix} (4.11') \\ (4.11'') \end{matrix}$$

Assume $L_F = 0$

$$L_H = \begin{Bmatrix} 1 \\ 0 \end{Bmatrix} \Leftrightarrow (\pi^M - \pi^D)\, p_2\, (2 - p_2) + p_2 \begin{Bmatrix} \geq \\ < \end{Bmatrix} 1 \qquad \begin{matrix} (4.12') \\ (4.12'') \end{matrix}$$

Subgame equilibria in period 1

$(0, 0)$

$$\pi^D (2 - p_2) - 1 < \pi^D (2 - p_2) \qquad (4.10'')$$

$$\wedge\ (\pi^M - \pi^D)\, p_2\, (2 - p_2) + p_2 < 1 \qquad (4.12'')$$

This condition cannot be met when equation 4.4' from period 2 is taken into account.

$(0, 1)$

$$\pi^D (2 - p_2) - 1 \geq \pi^D (2 - p_2) \qquad (4.10')$$

$$(\pi^M - \pi^D)\, p_1\, (2 - p_2) + p_2 < 1 \qquad (4.11'')$$

This is not a possible outcome because 4.10' can never be fulfilled.

$(1, 0)$

$$(2 - p_2)(p_2 - p_1)\, \pi^D < 1 \qquad (4.9'')$$

$$(\pi^M - \pi^D)\, p_2\, (2 - p_2) + p_2 \geq 1 \qquad (4.12')$$

Both equations can be fulfilled simultaneously.

$(1, 1)$

$$(2 - p_2)(p_2 - p_1)\, \pi^D \geq 1 \qquad (4.9')$$

$$(\pi^M - \pi^D)\, p_1\, (2 - p_2) + p_2 \geq 1 \qquad (4.11')$$

Both equations can be fulfilled simultaneously. There is also the possibility of no subgame equilibrium in period 1 being subject to the subgame equilibrium (1, 0) in period 2.

Subgame Equilibrium in Period 2: (1, 1)

The firms' reaction equations

U_F
Assume $L_H = 1$

$$L_F = \begin{Bmatrix} 1 \\ 0 \end{Bmatrix} \Leftrightarrow \pi^D\,(p_2 - p_1)\,(2 - p_1) - p_2 + p_1 \begin{Bmatrix} \geq \\ < \end{Bmatrix} 1 \qquad \begin{matrix} (4.13') \\ (4.13'') \end{matrix}$$

Assume $L_H = 0$

$$L_F = \begin{Bmatrix} 1 \\ 0 \end{Bmatrix} \Leftrightarrow \pi^D\,(2 - p_1) - 1 \begin{Bmatrix} \geq \\ < \end{Bmatrix} \pi^D\,(2 - p_1) \qquad \begin{matrix} (4.14') \\ (4.14'') \end{matrix}$$

U_H
Assume $L_F = 1$

$$L_H = \begin{Bmatrix} 1 \\ 0 \end{Bmatrix} \Leftrightarrow (\pi^M - \pi^D)\, p_1\, (2 - p_1) + p_1 \begin{Bmatrix} \geq \\ < \end{Bmatrix} 1 \qquad \begin{matrix} (4.15') \\ (4.15'') \end{matrix}$$

Assume $L_F = 0$

$$L_H = \begin{Bmatrix} 1 \\ 0 \end{Bmatrix} \Leftrightarrow (\pi^M - \pi^D)\, p_2\, (2 - p_1) + p_2 \begin{Bmatrix} \geq \\ < \end{Bmatrix} 1 \qquad \begin{matrix} (4.16') \\ (4.16'') \end{matrix}$$

Subgame equilibria in period 1

(0, 0)

$$\pi^D\,(2 - p_1) - 1 < \pi^D\,(2 - p_1) \qquad (4.14'')$$

$$(\pi^M - \pi^D)\, p_2\, (2 - p_1) + p_2 < 1 \qquad (4.16'')$$

These conditions, together with 4.3' from period 2 cannot be fulfilled simultaneously.

(0, 1)

$$\pi^D (2 - p_1) - 1 \geq \pi^D (2 - p_1) \qquad (4.14')$$

$$(\pi^M - \pi^D)\, p_1 (2 - p_1) + p_1 < 1 \qquad (4.15'')$$

This is not a possible outcome because condition (4.14') can never be met.

(1, 0)

$$\pi^D (p_2 - p_1)(2 - p_1) - p_2 + p_1 < 1 \qquad (4.13'')$$

$$(\pi^M - \pi^D)\, p_2 (2 - p_1) + p_2 \geq 1 \qquad (4.16')$$

These conditions, together with 4.1' and 4.3' from period 2, cannot be met for $p_1 < 1$.

(1, 1)

$$\pi^D (p_2 - p_1)(2 - p_1) - p_2 + p_1 \geq 1 \qquad (4.13')$$

$$(\pi^M - \pi^D)\, p_1 (2 - p_1) + p_1 \geq 1 \qquad (4.15')$$

The conditions can be met simultaneously.

Bibliography

Agell, J. and P. Lundborg (1995), 'Fair Wages in the Open Economy', *Economica,* **62** (247), pp. 335–51.

Aidt, T. (1998), 'Political Internalization of Economic Externalities and Environmental Policies', *Journal of Public Economics,* **69** (1), pp. 1–16.

Albert, M. and J. Meckl (1997), *Efficiency Wages, Unemployment and Welfare: A Trade Theorist's Guide,* University of Konstanz, Dept of Economics, Working Paper No. 348, Konstanz.

American Samoa Government (1994), *American Samoa – Statistical Digest,* Pago Pago: American Samoa Government, Economic Development Planning Office.

Appelbaum, E. and E. Katz (1986), 'Transfer Seeking and Avoidance: On the Full Social Costs of Rent Seeking', *Public Choice,* **48** (2), pp. 175–81.

Arden-Clarke, C. (1991), *The General Agreement on Tariffs and Trade, Environmental Protection and Sustainable Development,* Gland: World Wide Fund for Nature.

Associated Press (1995), 'Tuna Plant Closed', Available online: http: //www. lsu.edu/guests/sglegal/public_htm/fishum/fishum.jun95 (8 March 1997).

Austen Smith, D. (1991), 'Rational Consumers and Irrational Voters: A Review Essay on Black Hole Tariffs and Endogenous Policy Theory', *Economics and Politics,* **3** (1), pp. 73–92.

Bagwell, K. and R. Staiger (1992), 'The Sensitivity of Strategic and Corrective R&D Policy in Battles for Monopoly', *International Economic Review,* **33** (4), pp. 795–816.

Bagwell, K. and R. Staiger (1994), 'The Sensitivity of Strategic and Corrective R&D Policy in Oligopolistic Industries', *Journal of International Economics,* **36** (1–2), pp. 133–50.

Baik, K. and J. Shogren (1992), 'Strategic Behavior in Contests: Comment', *American Economic Review,* **82** (1), 359–62.

Baldwin, R. (1969), 'The Case Against Infant-Industry Tariff Protection', *Journal of Political Economy,* **77**, pp. 295–305.

Baldwin, R. and P. Krugman (1988), 'Market Access and Competition: A Simulation Study of 16K Random Access Memories', in R. Feenstra (ed), *Empirical Research in Industrial Trade,* Cambridge/Mass.: MIT Press, pp. 171–97.

Barrett, S. (1994), 'Strategic Environmental Policy and International Trade', *Journal of Public Economics,* **54** (3), pp. 325–38.

Bartsch, E. *et al.* (1993), *Environmental Regulation and the Impact of Lobbying Activities,* Kiel Institute of World Economics, Working Paper No. 562, Kiel.

Batra, R. (1971a), 'Factor Market Imperfections and Gains from Trade', *Oxford Economic Papers,* **23** (2), pp. 182–88.

Batra, R. (1971b), 'Factor Market Imperfections, the Terms of Trade and Welfare', *American Economic Review,* **61** (5), pp. 946–55.

Becker, G. (1976), 'Toward a More General Theory of Regulation: Comment', *Journal of Law and Economics,* **19** (2), pp. 245–48.

Bhagwati, J. (1971), 'The Generalized Theory of Distortions and Welfare', in: J. Bhagwati, R. Mudell and R. Jones (eds), *Trade, Balance of Payments and Growth: Papers in International Economics in Honor of Charles P. Kindleberger,* Amsterdam: North-Holland, pp. 69–90.

Bhagwati, J. (1982), 'Directly Unproductive, Profit-seeking (DUP) Activities', *Journal of Political Economy,* **90** (5), pp. 988–1002.

Bhagwati, J. (1995), 'Trade Liberalisation and "Fair Trade" Demands: Addressing the Environmental and Labour Standards Issues', *World Economy,* **18** (6), pp. 745–59.

Bhagwati, J. and V. Ramaswami (1963), 'Domestic Distortions, Tariffs and the Theory of Optimum Subsidy', *Journal of Political Economy,* **71**, pp. 44–50.

Bhagwati, J. and T. Srinivasan (1980), 'Revenue Seeking: A Generalization of the Theory of Tariffs', *Journal of Political Economy,* **88** (6), pp. 1069–87.

Black, D. (1958): *Theory of Committees and Elections,* Cambridge: Cambridge University Press.

Bommer, R. (1999), Environmental Policy and Industrial Competitiveness: The Pollution Haven Hypothesis Reconsidered', *Review of International Economics, of International Economics,* **7** (2), pp. 342–56.

Bommer, R. and G. Schulze (1999), 'Environmental Improvement with Trade Liberalization', *European Journal of Political Economy,* **15** (4), pp. 639–61.

Bonanno, A. and D. Constance (1996), *Caught in the Net – The Global Tuna Industry, Environmentalism, and the State,* Lawrence/Kansas: University of Kansas Press.

Brander, J. (1995), 'Strategic Trade Policy', in G. Grossman and K. Rogoff (eds), *Handbook of International Economics,* Vol. **3,** Amsterdam, Lausanne, New York, Oxford, Shannon, Tokyo: Elsevier, pp. 1395–445.

Brander, J. and B. Spencer (1983), 'Strategic Commitment with R&D: The Symmetric Case', *Bell Journal of Economics,* **14** (1), pp. 225–35.

Brander, J. and B. Spencer (1985), 'Export Subsidies and Market Share Rivalry', *Journal of International Economics,* **18**, pp. 83–100.

Brecher, R. (1974), 'Optimal Commercial Policy for a Minimum-Wage Economy', *Journal of International Economics,* **4** (2), pp. 139–49.

Bremer, H. (1982), 'Die zweite Schlacht von Poitiers', *Zeit,* **37,** 19 November 1982, p. 21.

Bronars, S. and J. Lott, Jr. (1994), *Do Campaign Donations Alter How Politicians Vote?,* University of Western Ontario, Working Paper, Dept. of Political Economy, No. 45.

Brown, D. *et al.* (1996), 'International Labor: Standards and Trade: A Theoretical Analysis', in J. Bhagwati and R. Hudec (eds), *Fair Trade and Harmonization,* Cambridge/Mass., London: MIT Press, pp. 225–80.

Buchanan, J. and G. Tullock (1975), 'Polluters' Profits and Political Response: Direct Controls Versus Taxes', *American Economic Review,* **65** (1), pp. 139–47.

Bulow, J. and L. Summers (1986), 'A Theory of Dual Labor Markets with Application to Industrial Policy, Discrimination, and Keynesian Unemployment', *Journal of Labor Economics,* **4** (3), pp. 376–414.

Burney, D. (1988a), 'Letter to David Burke, Executive Vice President, ABC-News from 24 March 1988', in US Senate, Committee on Commerce, Science, and Transportation, *Hearing on the Reauthorization of the Marine Mammal Protection Act,* Washington, DC: Government Printing Office, pp. 135–6.

Burney, D. (1988b), 'Statement on Behalf of the US Tuna Foundation', in US Senate, Committee on Commerce, Science, and Transportation, *The Reauthorization of the Marine Mammal Protection Act,* Washington, DC: Government Printing Office, pp. 136–7.

Burton, J. (1989), 'Lease of Shelf-life – Asian Food Suppliers are Buying their US Customers', *Far Eastern Economic Review,* **145,** 7 September 1989, pp. 108–109.

Cassing, J. and A. Hillman (1985), 'Political Influence Motives and the Choice between Tariffs and Quotas', *Journal of International Economics,* **19,** pp. 279–90.

Cassing, J. and A. Hillman (1986) 'Shifting Comparative Advantage and Senescent Industry Collapse', *American Economic Review,* **76,** pp. 516–23.

Charnovitz, S. (1991),'Exploring the Environmental Exceptions of GATT Article XX', *Journal of World Trade,* **25,** pp. 37–53.

Charnovitz, S. (1992), 'Environmental and Labour Standards in Trade', *World Economy,* **15** (3), pp. 335–56.

Cleeton, D. (1989), 'Equilibrium Conditions for Efficient Rent Seeking: The Nash–Cournot Solution', *Quarterly Review of Economics and Business,* **29** (2), pp. 6–14.

Clinton, W. (1998), *United States – Statement by H. E. Mr. William J. Clinton, President,* Available online: http://www.wto.org/wto/anniv /clinton.htm (22 June 1998), Geneva: WTO.

Colson, D. (1992), 'US Policy on Tuna–Dolphin Issues', *US Department of State Dispatch*, **3**, p. 15.

Conrad, K. (1993), 'Taxes and Subsidies for Pollution-Intensive Industries as Trade Policy', *Journal of Environmental Economics and Management*, **25** (2), pp. 121–35.

Conrad, K. (1996), 'Choosing Emission Taxes under International Price Competition', in C. Carraro, Y. Katsoulacos and A. Xepapadeas (eds), *Environmental Policy and Market Structure*, Amsterdam: Kluwer, pp. 85–98.

Corden, W. (1984), 'The Normative Theory of International Trade', in R. Jones and P. Kenen (eds), *Handbook of International Economics*, **1**, Amsterdam, New York, Oxford: North-Holland, pp. 63–130.

Corden, W. (1989), *Trade Policy and Economic Welfare*, Oxford: Oxford University Press.

CQ-Almanac (1972), 'Congress Approves Moratorium on Sea Mammal Killing', *Congressional Quarterly Almanac*, **90**, pp. 961–9.

CQ-Almanac (1977), 'Tuna–Porpoise Controversy', *Congressional Quarterly Almanac*, **95**, p. 674.

Daly, H. (1992), 'Free-Market Environmentalism: Turning a Good Servant into a Bad Master', *Critical Review*, **6** (2–3), 171–83.

Daly, H. (1995), 'Against Free Trade: Neoclassical and Steady-State Perspectives', *Journal of Evolutionary Economics*, **5** (3), pp. 313–26.

Dasgupta, P. (1986), 'The Theory of Technological Competition', in J. Stiglitz and G. Mathewson (eds), *New Developments in the Analysis of Market Structure: Proceedings of a Conference held by the International Economic Association in Ottawa, Canada*, Cambridge/Mass.: MIT Press; London: Macmillan Press, pp. 519–27.

Dasgupta, P. and J. Stiglitz (1988), 'Learning-by-doing, Market Structure and Industrial and Trade Policies', *Oxford Economic Papers*, **40**, 246–68.

Davidson, C. (1984), 'Cartel Stability and Trade Policy', *Journal of International Economics*, **17**, pp. 219–37.

Davis, O. *et al.* (1970): 'An Expository Development of a Mathematical Model of the Electoral Process', *American Political Science Review*, **64** (2), pp. 426–48.

Declaration of Panama (1995), Available online: http://www.greenpeace. org/~usa/campaigns/biodiversity/panama.html (14 March 1997).

Dixit, A. (1987), 'Strategic Behavior in Contests', *American Economic Review*, **77** (5), pp. 891–8.

Dixit, A. (1996), *The Making of Economic Policy: A Transaction Cost Politics Perspective*, Cambridge/Mass. and London: MIT Press.

Dixit, A. and V. Norman (1980), *Theory of International Trade*, Cambridge: Cambridge University Press.

Doulman, D. and R. Kearney (1987), 'Domestic Tuna Industries', in D. Doulman (ed), *The Development of the Tuna Industry in the Pacific*

Island Region: An Analysis of Options, Honolulu/Hawaii: East–West Center, pp. 3–32.

Downs, A. (1957), *An Economic Theory of Democracy*, New York: Harper & Row.

Drèze, J. and N. Stern (1987), 'The Theory of Cost-Benefit Analysis', in A. Auerbach, J. and M. Feldstein (eds), *Handbook of Public Economics*, Amsterdam, New York, Oxford, Tokyo: North-Holland, pp. 909–89.

Eaton, J. and G. Grossman (1986), 'Optimal Trade and Industrial Policy under Oligopoly', *Quarterly Journal of Economics*, **101** (2), pp. 383–406.

Economist (1993a), 'Don't Green the GATT', *Economist*, **343**, 26 December 1993, pp. 15–16.

Economist (1993b), 'The Greening of Protectionism', *Economist*, **343**, 27 February 1993, pp. 19–21.

Economist (1994), 'Regulate Us, Please!', *Economist*, **344**, 8 January 1994, p. 65.

Economist (1995), 'Shell on the Rocks', *Economist*, **345**, 24 June 1995, pp. 67–8.

Enelow, J. and M. Hinich (1984), *The Spatial Theory of Voting*, Cambridge, London, New York, New Rochelle, Melbourne, Sydney: Cambridge University Press.

Esty, D. (1994), *Greening the GATT*, Washington, DC: Institute of International Economics.

Ethier, W. (1982), 'National and International Returns to Scale in the Modern Theory of International Trade', *American Economic Review*, **72** (4), pp. 389–405.

Felando, A. (1988), 'Statement on Behalf of the American Tunaboat Association', in US Senate, Committee on Commerce, Science, and Transportation, *The Reauthorization of the Marine Mammal Protection Act*, Washington, DC: Government Printing Office, pp. 100–17.

Findlay, R. and S. Wellisz (1982), 'Endogenous Tariffs, the Political Economy of Trade Restrictions, and Welfare', in J. Bhagwati (ed), *Import Competition and Response*, Chicago, London: University of Chicago Press.

Finger, J. *et al.* (1982), 'The Political Economy of Administered Protection', *American Economic Review*,**72** (3), pp. 452–66.

Floyd, J. (1987), 'US Tuna Import Regulations', in D. Doulman (ed), *The Development of the Tuna Industry in the Pacific Island Region: An Analysis of Options*, Honolulu/Hawaii: East–West Center, pp. 81–90.

Food and Agriculture Organization (1994*), FAO Yearbook: Fishery Statistics – Catches and Landings*, Rome: FAO.

Food and Agriculture Organization (1995), *FAO Yearbook: Fishery Statistics – Catches and Landings*, Rome: FAO.

Fudenberg, D. and J. Tirole (1993), *Game Theory*, Cambridge/Mass.: MIT Press.

Fung, K. (1994), 'Book Review: *Empirical Studies of Strategic Trade Policy* by Paul Krugman and Alasdair Smith', *Journal of Economic Literature,* **32**, pp. 1891–93.

General Agreement on Tariffs and Trade (1982), *United States – Prohibition on the Import of Tuna and Tuna Products from Canada – Report of the Panel,* BISD 29/S/91-109, Geneva: GATT.

General Agreement on Tariffs and Trade (1987), *United States – Taxes on Petroleum and other Environmental Taxes – Report of the Panel,* BISD 24/S/136-166, Geneva: GATT.

General Agreement on Tariffs and Trade (1988), *Canada – Restrictions on Exports of Unprocessed Herring and Salmon – Report of the Panel,* BISD 35/S/98-115, Geneva: GATT.

General Agreement on Tariffs and Trade (1990), *Thailand – Restriction on the Importation of Cigarettes – Report of the Panel,* BISD 37/S/200-228, Geneva: GATT.

General Agreement on Tariffs and Trade (1991*), United States – Restrictions on Imports of Tuna – Report of the Panel,* GATT-Document DS21/R, Geneva: GATT.

General Agreement on Tariffs and Trade (1992), *International Trade 90–91,* Geneva: GATT.

General Agreement on Tariffs and Trade (1994a), 'United States – Restrictions on Tuna – Report of the Panel', in J. Cameron, P. Demaret and D. Gerardin (eds), *Trade & Environment – The Search for the Balance,* **2**, London: Cameron May.

General Agreement on Tariffs and Trade (1994b*), United States – US Taxes on Automobiles – Report of the Panel,* GATT-Document DS31/R, Geneva: GATT.

Gialloretto, L. (1989), 'Selective Regulation: A Trend of the 90s', *The Avmark Aviation Economist,* **10**, pp. 15–17.

Goldberg, D. (1994a), *GATT Tuna–Dolphin II: Environmental Protection Continues to Clash with Free Trade – Part I,* Available online: http://www.econet. apc.org/ciel/issue2.html (8 November 1996), Geneva: Center for International Environmental Law.

Goldberg, D. (1994b), *GATT Tuna–Dolphin II: Environmental Protection Continues to Clash with Free Trade – Part II,* Available online: http://www.econet.apc.org/ciel/issue2b.html (8 November 1996), Geneva: Center for International Environmental Law.

Goodland, R. and H. Daly (1996), 'If Tropical Log Export Bans Are So Perverse, Why Are There So Many?', *Ecological Economics,* **18** (3), pp. 189–96.

Gorz, A. (1987), *Farewell to the Working Class – An Essay on Post-Industrial Socialism,* London, Sydney: Pluto Press.

Graaff, J. (1949), 'On Optimum Tariff Structures', *Review of Economic Studies,* **17**, pp. 47–59.

Gradstein, M. (1995) 'Intensity of Competition, Entry and Entry Deterrence in Rent Seeking Contests', *Economics and Politics*, **7** (1), pp. 79–91.

Grossman, G. (1987), 'Strategic Export Promotion: A Critique', in P. Krugman (ed), *Strategic Trade Policy and the New International Economics*, Cambridge/Mass.: MIT Press, pp. 47–68.

Grossman, G. and E. Helpman (1994), 'Protection for Sale', *American Economic Review*, **84** (4), pp. 833–50.

Grossman, G. and E. Helpman (1995), 'Trade Wars and Trade Talks', *Journal of Political Economy*, **103** (4), pp. 675–708.

H.J. Heinz Company (1985), *Annual Report*, Pittsburgh: H.J. Heinz Company.

Haberler, G. (1950), 'Some Problems in the Pure Theory of International Trade', *Economic Journal*, **60**, pp. 223–40.

Hahn, R. (1989), *A Primer on Environmental Policy Design*, New York, London, Melbourne: Harwood Academic Publishers.

Hahn, R. (1990), 'The Political Economy of Environmental Regulation: Towards a Unifying Framework', *Public Choice*, **65** (1), pp. 21–47.

Hamilton, A. (1791), 'Report on Manufactures', in H. Lodge (ed) (1903), *The Work of Alexander Hamilton*, New York: Putnam, reprinted (1971) St. Clair Shores/Michigan: Scholarly Press, pp. 70–192.

Handelsblatt (1997), 'In Washington mehren sich japanfeindliche Töne', *Handelsblatt*, **29** (189), p. 2.

Handley, P. (1989), 'Unicord's Big Catch – Thailand's Tuna Giant goes Fishing in the US', *Far Eastern Economic Review*, **145**, 7 September 1989, p. 108.

Handley, P. (1991a), 'Off the Hook', *Far Eastern Economic Review*, **147**, 23 May 1991, pp. 48–50.

Handley, P. (1991b), 'Row of Canneries', *Far Eastern Economic Review*, **147**, 23 May 1991, p. 48.

Hanson, G. (1983), *Social Clauses and International Trade: An Economic Analysis of Labor Standards in Trade Policy*, New York: St. Martin's Press.

Harris, J. and M. Todaro (1970), 'Migration, Unemployment & Development: A Two-Sector Analysis', *American Economic Review*, **60** (1), pp. 126–42.

Harrison, A. (1994), 'An Empirical Test of the Infant Industry Argument: Comment', *American Economic Review*, **84** (4), pp. 1090–95.

Head, K. (1994) 'Infant Industry Protection in the Steel Rail Industry', *Journal of International Economics*, **37**, pp. 141–65.

Helpman, E. (1981), 'International Trade in the Presence of Product Differentiation, Economies of Scale, and Monopolistic Competition – a Chamberlin-Heckscher-Ohlin Approach', *Journal of International Economics*, **11**, pp. 305–40.

Helpman, E. (1984), 'Increasing Returns, Imperfect Markets, and Trade Theory', in R. Jones and P. Kenen (eds), *Handbook of International Economics*, **1**, New York, Amsterdam, Oxford: Elsevier, pp. 325–65.

Herberg, H. and M. Kemp (1971), 'Factor Market Distortions, the Shape of the Locus of Competitive Outputs, and the Relation between Product Prices and Equilibrium Outputs', in J. Bhagwati, R. Mudell and R. Jones (eds), *Trade, Balance of Payments and Growth: Papers in International Economics in Honor of Charles P. Kindleberger*, Amsterdam: North-Holland, pp. 22–48.

Herberg, H. *et al.* (1982), 'Further Implications of Variable Returns to Scale', *Journal of International Economics,* **13** (1–2), pp. 65–84.

Hillman, A. (1977), 'The Brigden Theorem: The Inefficiency of Tariffs, Public Sophistication and the Merit-Want Market Failure', *Economic Record*, **53** (142–143), pp. 434–46.

Hillman, A. (1982), 'Declining Industries and Political-Support Protectionist Motives', *American Economic Review*, **72** (5), pp. 1180–87.

Hillman, A. (1989), *The Political Economy of Protection*, Chur: Harwood Academic Publishers.

Hillman, A. (1992), 'International Trade Policy: Benevolent Dictators and Optimizing Politicians', *Public Choice*, **74**, pp. 1–15.

Hillman, A. and P. Moser (1996), 'Trade Liberalization as Politically Optimal Exchange of Market Access', in M. Canzoneri, W. Ethier and V. Grilli (eds), *The New Transatlantic Order,* Cambridge: Cambridge University Press, pp. 295–311.

Hillman, A. and J. Riley (1989), 'Politically Contestable Rents and Transfers', *Economics and Politics,* **1** (1), pp. 17–39.

Hillman, A. and D. Samet (1987), 'Dissipation of Contestable Rents by Small Numbers of Contenders', *Public Choice,* **54** (1), pp. 63–82.

Hillman, A. and H. Ursprung (1988), 'Domestic Politics, Foreign Interests, and International Trade Policy', *American Economic Review,* **78** (4), pp. 719–45.

Hillman, A. and H. Ursprung (1992), 'The Influence of Environmental Concerns on the Political Determination of Trade Policy', in K. Anderson and R. Blackhurst (eds), *The Greening of World Trade Issues*, New York, London, Toronto, Sydney, Tokyo, Singapore: Harvester Wheatsheaf, pp. 195–220.

Hillman, A. and H. Ursprung (1994a), 'Greens, Supergreens, and International Trade Policy', in C. Carraro (ed), *Trade, Innovation, Environment*, Dordrecht: Kluwer Academic Publishers, pp. 75–108.

Hillman, A. and H. Ursprung (1994b), 'Domestic Politics, Foreign Interests, and International Trade Policy: Reply', *American Economic Review*, **84** (5), pp. 1476–8.

Hirshleifer, J. (1989), 'Conflict and Rent-Seeking Success Functions: Ratio vs. Difference Models of Relative Success', *Public Choice,* **63** (2), pp. 101–12.

Hirshleifer, J. (1995), 'Theorizing About Conflict', in K. Hartley (ed), *Handbook of Defence Economics,* Amsterdam: Elsevier, pp. 165–89.

Hirshleifer, J. and J. Riley (1978), *Auctions and Contests*, UCLA, Working Paper No. 118b, Los Angeles.

Hoekman, B. and M. Leidy (1992), 'Environmental Policy Formation in a Trading Economy: A Public Choice Perspective', in: K. Anderson and R. Blackhurst (eds), *The Greening of World Trade Issues*, New York, London, Toronto, Sydney, Tokyo, Singapore: Harvester Wheatsheaf, pp. 221–46.

Hood, G. (1995), 'Windy Craggy: An Analysis of Environmental Interest Group and Mining Industry Approaches', *Resources Policy*, **21** (1), pp. 13–20.

Horstmann, I. and J. Markusen (1986), 'Up the Average Cost Curve: Inefficient Entry and the New Protectionism', *Journal of International Economics*, **20** (3–4), pp. 225–47.

Hotelling, H. (1929), 'Stability in Competition', *Economic Journal,* **39**, pp. 41–57.

Hudgins, L. (1987), 'The Development of the Mexican Tuna Industry, 1976–1986', in D. Doulman (ed), *The Development of the Tuna Industry in the Pacific Islands Region: An Analysis of Options,* Honolulu/Hawaii: East–West Center, pp. 153–68.

Hufbauer, G. *et al.* (1990), *Economic Sanctions Reconsidered*, Washington, DC: Institute for International Economics.

Inter-American Tropical Tuna Commission (1981*), Annual Report 1980,* La Jolla/California: IATTC.

Inter-American Tropical Tuna Commission (1984*), Annual Report 1983,* La Jolla/California: IATTC.

Inter-American Tropical Tuna Commission (1985), *Annual Report 1984*, La Jolla/California: IATTC.

Inter-American Tropical Tuna Commission (1993*), Annual Report 1992,* La Jolla/California: IATTC.

Japan Times (1996), 'US will Try to Change Tuna Import Rules in 1997', *Japan Times,* 30 October 1996, p. 22.

Johnson, H. (1951), 'Optimum Welfare and Maximum Revenue Tariffs', *Review of Economic Studies,* **19**, pp. 28–35.

Johnson, H. (1954), 'Optimum Tariffs and Retaliation', *Review of Economic Studies,* **21**(4), pp. 142–53.

Johnson, H. (1965), 'Optimal Trade Intervention in the Presence of Domestic Distortions', in R. Caves, H. Johnson and P. Kenen (eds), *Trade, Growth, and the Balance of Payments – Essays in Honor of Gottfried Haberler*, Chicago: Rand McNally, pp. 3–34.

Joseph, J. (1988), 'Letter of Dr. James Joseph, Director of the Inter-American Tropical Tuna Commission, to Senator Ernest Hollings from 27 April 1988', in US Senate, Committee on Commerce, Science, and Transportation, *Hearings on the Reauthorization of the Marine Mammal Protection Act,* Washington, DC: Government Printing Office, pp. 135–6.

Joseph, J. (1996), 'Testimony on the International Dolphin Conservation Act and the International Dolphin Protection Consumer Information Act', in US House of Representatives, *Hearing on the International Dolphin Conservation Act and the International Dolphin Protection Consumer Information Act,* Washington, DC: Government Printing Office, pp. 322–38.

Kaempfer, W. and A. Lowenberg (1992), *International Economic Sanctions: A Public Choice Perspective,* Boulder/Colorado: Westview Press.

Kaldor, N. (1940), 'A Note on Tariffs and the Terms of Trade', *Economica,* 7, pp. 377–80.

Kemp, M. (1960), 'The Mill-Bastable Infant-Industry Dogma', *Journal of Political Economy,* 68, pp. 65–7.

Kennedy, P. (1994), 'Equilibrium Pollution Taxes in Open Economies with Imperfect Competition', *Journal of Environmental Economics and Management,* 27 (1), pp. 49–63.

King, D. (1987), 'The US Tuna Market: A Pacific Islands Perspective', in D. Doulman (ed), *The Development of the Tuna Industry in the Pacific Island Region: An Analysis of Options,* Honolulu/Hawaii: East–West Center, pp. 63–79.

Körber, A. (1995), 'Standards and Taxes in Environmental Law from a Public Choice Perspective', in B. Bouckaert and G. De Geest (eds), *Essays in Law and Economics II,* Antwerp: Maklu, pp. 161–91.

Körber, A. (1998), 'Why Everybody Loves Flipper: A Political Economic Analysis of the US Dolphin Safe Legislation', *European Journal of Political Economy,* 14 (3), pp. 475–509.

Körber, A. and M. Kolmar (1996), 'To Fight or Not to Fight? An Analysis of Submission, Struggle, and the Design of Contests', *Public Choice,* 88 (3–4), pp. 381–92.

Krueger, A. (1974), 'The Political Economy of the Rent-Seeking Society', *American Economic Review,* 64 (3), pp. 291–303.

Krueger, A. and B. Tuncer (1982), 'An Empirical Test of the Infant Industry Argument', *American Economic Review,* 72 (5), pp. 1142–52.

Krueger, A. and B. Tuncer (1994), 'An Empirical Test of the Infant Industry Argument: Reply', *American Economic Review,* 84 (4), p. 1096.

Krugman, P. (1979), 'Increasing Returns, Monopolistic Competition, and International Trade', *Journal of International Economics,* 9, pp. 469–79.

Krugman, P. (1980), 'Scale Economies, Product Differentiation, and the Pattern of Trade', *American Economic Review,* 70, pp. 950–59.

Krugman, P. (1981), 'Intraindustry Specialization and the Gains from Trade', *Journal of Political Economy,* 89, pp. 959–73.

Krugman, P. (1987), 'Is Free Trade Passé?', *Journal of Economic Perspectives,* **1** (2), pp. 131–44.

Krugman, P. and A. Smith (eds) (1994), *Empirical Studies of Strategic Trade Policy*, Chicago: University of Chicago Press.

LaBudde, S. (1988), 'Testimony on Behalf of the Earth Island Institute', in US Senate, Committee on Commerce, Science, and Transportation: *Hearings on the Reauthorization of the Marine Mammal Protection Act*, Washington, DC: Government Printing Office, pp. 98–103.

Lancaster, K. (1980), 'Intra-industry trade under perfect monopolistic competition', *Journal of International Economics,* **10**, pp. 151–75.

Laplante, B. and J. Garbutt (1992), 'Environmental Protectionism', *Land Economics*, **68** (1), pp. 116–19.

Lash, S. and J. Urry (1987), *The End of Organized Capitalism*, Oxford: Basil Blackwell.

Leininger, W. (1991), 'Patent Competition, Rent Dissipation, and the Persistence of Monopoly: The Role of Research Budgets', *Journal of Economic Theory*, **53** (1), pp. 146–72.

Lerner, A. (1934), 'The Diagrammatical Representation of Demand Conditions in International Trade', *Economica*, **1**, 319–34.

Lerner, A. (1944), *The Economics of Control*, New York: Macmillan.

Linse, U. (1986), *Ökopax und Anarchie: Eine Geschichte der ökologischen Bewegung in Deutschland*, Munich: dtv.

Linster, B. (1993), 'Stackelberg Rent-Seeking', *Public Choice*, **77** (2), pp. 307–21.

Lipsey, R. and K. Lancaster (1956), 'The General Theory of the Second Best', *Review of Economic Studies*, **24**, pp. 11–32.

List, F. (1841), *Das Nationale System der Politischen Ökonomie*, reprinted in G. Fabiunke (ed) (1982), *Das Nationale System der Politischen Ökonomie*, Berlin: Akademie-Verlag.

Long, N. and N. Vousden (1991), 'Protectionist Responses and Declining Industries', *Journal of International Economics*, **30** (1–2), pp. 87–103.

Los Angeles Times (1995), 'Tuna Wholesaler seeks to Buy Cannery', *Los Angeles Times*, 23. December 1995, p. 2

Luzio, E. and S. Greenstein (1995), 'Measuring the Performance of a Protected Infant Industry: The Case of Brazilian Microcomputers', *Review of Economics and Statistics*, **77** (4), pp. 622–33.

McArthur, J. and S. Marks (1988), 'Constituent Interest vs. Legislative Ideology: The Role of Political Opportunity Cost', *Economic Inquiry*, **26**, pp. 461–70.

McCubbins, M. and T. Page (1986), 'The Congressional Foundations of Agency Performance', *Public Choice*, **51** (2), pp. 173–90.

Magee, S. (1988), 'Optimal Obfuscation and the Theory of the Second-Worst: A Theory of Public Choice', in S. Magee, W. Brock and L. Young (eds), *Endogenous Policy Theory*, Cambridge: Cambridge University Press.

Magee, S, W. Brock and L. Young (eds) (1988), *Endogenous Policy Theory*, Cambridge: Cambridge University Press.

Magee, S. *et al.* (1989), 'Black Hole Tariff Endogenous Policy Theory', Cambridge, New York, Port Chester, Melbourne, Sydney: Cambridge University Press.

Maggi, G. (1996), 'Strategic Trade Policies with Endogenous Mode of Competition', *American Economic Review*, **86**, pp. 237–58.

Maloney, M. and R. McCormick (1982), 'A Positive Theory of Environmental Quality Regulation', *Journal of Law and Economics*, **25** (1), pp. 99–123.

Matusz, S. (1994), 'International Trade Policy in a Model of Unemployment and Wage Differentials', *Canadian Journal of Economics*, **27** (4), pp. 939–49.

Matusz, S. (1996), 'International Trade, the Division of Labor, and Unemployment', *International Economic Review*, **37** (1), pp. 71–84.

Mayer, W. (1984), 'Endogenous Tariff Formation', *American Economic Review*, **74** (5), pp. 970–85.

Mayer, W. and J. Li (1994), 'Interest Groups, Electoral Competition, and Probabilistic Voting for Trade Policies', *Economics and Politics*, **6** (1), pp. 59–77.

Meade, J. (1955), *Trade and Welfare*, London: Oxford University Press.

Melvin, J. and R. Warne (1973), 'Monopoly and the Theory of International Trade', *Journal of International Economics*, **3** (2), pp. 117–34.

Michaelis, P. (1994), 'Regulate Us, Please! On Strategic Lobbying in Cournot-Nash Oligopoly', *Journal of Institutional and Theoretical Economics*, **150** (4), pp. 693–709.

Mill, J. (1848), *Principles of Political Economy,* reprinted in J. Riley (ed) (1994), *Principles of Political Economy and Chapters on Socialism*, Oxford: Oxford University Press.

Mitchell, W. and M. Munger (1991), 'Economic Models of Interest Groups: An Introductory Survey'*, American Journal of Political Science*, **35**, pp. 512–46.

Mitsubishi Foods (MC) (1990), 'Letter of Mitsubishi Foods (MC) to David Phillips, Director of the Earth Island Institute, from 25 April 1990', in US House of Representatives, Committee on Merchant Marine and Fisheries, Subcommittee on Fisheries and Wildlife Conservation and the Environment, *Hearing on the International Dolphin Protection Consumer Information Act*, Washington, DC: Government Printing Office, pp. 325–6.

Muñoz, J. (1990), 'Statement on Behalf of van Camp Seafood', in US House of Representatives, Committee on Merchant Marine and Fisheries, Subcommittee on Fisheries, Wildlife Conservation, and the Environment,

Hearing on the International Dolphin Protection Consumer Information Act, Washington, DC: Government Printing Office.

National Research Council (1992), 'Dolphins and the Tuna Industry', National Research Council, Committee on Reducing Porpoise Mortality from Tuna Fishing, Board on Biology, Board on Environmental Studies and Toxicology, Commission on Life Sciences, Washington DC.

Neary, J. (1978), 'Short-Run Capital Specificity and the Pure Theory of International Trade', *Economic Journal*, **88** (351), pp. 488–510.

New York Times (1990), 'Dolphins and Double Hulls', *New York Times,* 14 April 1990, p. 22.

Nitzan, S. (1994), 'Modelling Rent-Seeking Contests', *European Journal of Political Economy*, **10**, pp. 41–60.

O'Reilly, A. (1990), 'Letter of Anthony J. F. O'Reilly to Rep. Barbara Boxer', in US House of Representatives, Committee on Merchant Marine and Fisheries, Subcommittee on Fisheries and Wildlife Conservation and the Environment, *Hearing on the International Dolphin Protection Consumer Information Act*, Washington, DC: Government Printing Office.

Olson, M. (1965), *The Logic of Collective Action – Public Goods and the Theory of Groups*, Cambridge/Mass.: Harvard University Press.

Organisation for Economic Co-operation and Development (1995a), *Trade, Environment and Development Co-operation*, Working Paper No. 45, Paris: OECD.

Organisation for Economic Co-operation and Development (1995b), *Eco-Labelling: Actual Effects of Selected Programmes*, OECD/GD (97) 105, Paris: OECD.

Organisation for Economic Co-operation and Development (1996a), *Antitrust and Market Access: The Scope and Coverage of Competition Laws and Implications for Trade*, Paris: OECD.

Organisation for Economic Co-operation and Development (1996b), *Trade, Employment and Labour Standards – A Study of Core Workers' Rights and International Trade*, Paris: OECD.

Organisation for Economic Co-operation and Development (1997), *Experience With the Use of Trade Measures in the Convention on International Trade in Endangered Species of Wild Fauna and Flora (CITES)*, OCDE/GD (97)106, Paris: OECD.

Oster, S. (1982), 'The Strategic Use of Regulatory Investment by Industry Sub-Groups', *Economic Inquiry*, **20** (4), pp. 604–18.

Panagariya, A. and D. Rodrik (1993), 'Political-Economy Arguments for a Uniform Tariff', *International Economic Review*, **34** (3), pp. 685–703.

Paul, C. and A. Wilhite (1994), 'Illegal Markets and the Social Costs of Rent-Seeking', *Public Choice*, **79** (1–2), pp. 105–15.

Peltzman, S. (1976), 'Toward a More General Theory of Regulation', *Journal of Law and Economics*, **19** (2), pp. 211–40.

Perez Castrillo, J. and T. Verdier (1992), 'A General Analysis of Rent-Seeking Games', *Public Choice*, **73** (3), pp. 335–50.

Petersmann, E. (1993), 'International Trade Law and International Environmental Law – Prevention and Settlement of International Environmental Disputes in GATT', *Journal of World Trade*, **27**, pp. 43–81.

Petersmann, E. (1995), *International and European Trade and Environmental Law after the Uruguay Round*, London, The Hague, Boston: Kluwer.

Petulla, J. (1980), *American Environmentalism - Values, Tactics, Priorities*, College Station, London: Texas A&M University Press.

Posner, R. (1975), 'The Social Costs of Monopoly and Regulation', *Journal of Political Economy*, **83** (4), pp. 807–27.

Ramirez, A. (1990), '"Epic Debate" Led to Heinz Tuna Plan –Telephone Interview with Anthony O'Reilly, CEO of H. J. Heinz', *New York Times*, 16 April 1990, p. D1.

Rauscher, M. (1992), 'Economic Integration and the Environment: Effects on Members and Non-members', *Environmental and Resource Economics*, **2**, pp. 221–36.

Rauscher, M. (1994), 'On Ecological Dumping', *Oxford Economic Papers*, **46** (5), pp. 822–40.

Rauscher, M. (1997), *International Trade, Factor Movement, and the Environment*, Oxford: Clarendon Press.

Riker, W. and P. Ordeshook (1993), 'A Theory of the Calculus of Voting', in C. Rowley (ed), *Public Choice Theory*, **1**, Aldershot, UK and Brookfield, US: Edward Elgar.

Rodrik, D. (1993), Taking Trade Policy Seriously: Export Subsidization as a Case Study in Policy Effectiveness, National Bureau of Economic Research (NBER), Working Paper No. 4567.

Rodrik, D. (1995), 'Political Economy of Trade Policy', in G. Grossman and K. Rogoff (eds), *Handbook of International Economics*, **3**, Amsterdam, Lausanne, New York, Oxford, Shannon, Tokyo: Elsevier.

Rotemberg, J. and G. Saloner (1989), 'Tariffs vs. Quotas with Implicit Collusion', *Canadian Journal of Economics*, **22**, pp. 237–44.

Rowley, C. (1988), 'Rent-Seeking Versus Directly Unproductive Profit-Seeking Activities', in C. Rowley, R. Tollinson and G. Tullock (eds), *The Political Economy of Rent-Seeking*, Boston, Dordrecht, Lancaster: Kluwer Academic Publishers, pp. 15–26.

Ruland, L. and J. Viaene (1993), 'The Political Choice of the Exchange Rate Regime', *Economics and Politics*, **5** (3), pp. 271–84.

Salop, S. and D. Scheffman (1983), 'Raising Rivals' Costs', *American Economic Review*, **73** (Papers & Proceedings), pp. 267–71.

Scheele, L. (1988), 'Statement on Behalf of Greenpeace', in US Senate, Committee on Commerce, Science, and Transportation, *Hearing on the*

Reauthorization of the Marine Mammal Protection Act, Washington, DC: Government Printing Office, pp. 105–11.

Schuknecht, L. (1992), *Trade Protection in the European Community*, Chur, Reading, Paris, Philadelphia, Tokyo, Melbourne: Harwood Academic Publishers.

Schulze, G and H. Ursprung (2000), 'The Political Economy of International Trade and the Environment', in G. Schulze and H. Ursprung (eds), *International Environmental Economics: A Survey of the Issues*, Oxford: Oxford University Press, forthcoming.

Schweinberger, A. (1978), 'Employment Subsidies and the Theory of Minimum Wage Rates in General Equilibrium', *Quarterly Journal of Economics*, **92** (3), pp. 361–74.

Schweinberger, A. (1995*), Environmental Policy, the Gains from Trade and the Double Dividend Debate*, University of Konstanz, Dept. of Economics, Working Paper No. 267.

Scitovsky, T. (1942), 'A Reconsideration of the Theory of Tariffs', *Review of Economic Studies*, **9,** pp. 89–110.

Seafood International (1988), 'Turn to Tuna', *Seafood International*, December 1988.

Shabecoff, P. (1990) '3 Companies to Stop Selling Tuna Netted with Dolphins', *New York Times*, 13 April 1990, p. 1.

Shrybman, S. (1993), 'Trading Away the Environment', in R. Grinspun and M. Cameron (eds), *The Political Economy of North American Free Trade*, New York: St. Martin's Press, pp. 271–94.

Skaperdas, S. (1996), 'Contest Success Functions', *Economic Theory*, 7, pp. 283–90.

Sorsa, P. (1995), *Environmental Protectionism, North–South Trade, and the Uruguay Round*, International Monetary Fund, Working Paper No. 5/6, Washington, DC.

StarKist (1996), *Heinz Plans to Acquire Additional US Tuna Production Facilities*, Available online: http://www.starkist.com/bbee.htm (27 January 1997), pp. 1–2.

Stephan, J. and H. Ursprung (1998), 'The Social Cost of Rent Seeking when Victories are Potentially Transient and Losses Final', in K. Koch and K. Jäger (eds), *Trade, Growth, and Economic Policy in Open Economies – Essays in Honour of Hans-Jürgen Vosgerau*, Berlin: Springer, pp. 369–80.

Stigler, G. (1971), 'The Theory of Economic Regulation', *Bell Journal of Economics and Management Science*, **2**, pp. 3–21.

Stratmann, T. (1991), 'What Do Campaign Contributions Buy? Deciphering Causal Effects of Money and Votes', *Southern Economic Journal*, **57** (3), pp. 55–77.

Studds, G. (1990), 'Question of Rep. Gerry Studds', in US House of Representatives, Committee on Merchant Marine and Fisheries, Subcommittee on Fisheries and Wildlife Conservation and the Environment, *Hearing on the International Dolphin Consumer Information Act*, Washington DC: Government Printing Office, p. 53.

Tagesanzeiger (1997), 'Verbot für lärmigste Jets', *Tagesanzeiger*, 21 October 1997, p. 5.

Time (1982), 'Protectionist Tide – In Geneva Delegates Gather for a Slanging Match', *Time*, pp. 26–27.

Tollinson, R. and R. Congleton (eds) (1995), *The Economic Analysis of Rent Seeking*, International Library of Critical Writings in Economics, Aldershot, UK and Brookfield, US: Edward Elgar.

Tullock, G. (1967), 'The Welfare Costs of Tariffs, Monopolies, and Theft', *Western Economic Journal*, **5**, pp. 224–32.

Tullock, G. (1980), 'Efficient Rent-Seeking', in J. Buchanan, R. Tollinson and G. Tullock (eds), *Towards a Theory of the Rent-Seeking Society*, College Station: Texas A&M University Press, pp. 97–112.

Ulph, A. (1992), 'The Choice of Environmental Policy Instruments and Strategic International Trade', in R. Pethig (ed), *Conflicts and Cooperation in Managing Environmental Resources*, Berlin: Springer.

Ulph, A. (1994), *Environmental Policy – A Survey of Recent Economic Analysis*, Fondazione Eni Enrico Mattei, Working Paper No. 53.94, Milan.

Ulph, A. (1996) 'Environmental Policy and International Trade When Governments and Producers Act Strategically', *Journal of Environmental Economics and Management*, **30** (3), pp. 265–81.

United Nations (1997), *Earth Summit + 5*, Available online: http:// www.un. org/dpcsd/earthsummit/ (19 December 1997), New York: UN-Dept. of Economic and Social Affairs.

Ursprung, H. (1988), 'Die Einführung politischer Elemente in die Theorie der internationalen Handelspolitik: Einige neuere Ergebnisse', *Geld und Währung*, pp. 28–44.

Ursprung, H. (1990), 'Public Goods, Rent Dissipation, and Candidate Competition', *Economics and Politics,* **2** (2): pp. 115–32.

Ursprung, H. (1992*), The Political Economy of Environmental Decision-making*, University of Konstanz, Dept of Economics, Working Paper No. 176, Konstanz.

US District Court-N.D. California (1990*), Earth Island Institute v. Robert Mosbacher et al.,* US District Court, N.D. California, C-88-1380-TEH28.

US International Trade Commission (1986), *Competitive Conditions in the US Tuna Industry – Report to the President on Investigation No. 332–224 under Section 332 (g) of the Tariff Act of 1930 as Amended*, USITC-Publication 1912, Washington, DC: USITC.

US International Trade Commission (1990), *Tuna: Competitive Conditions Affecting the US and European Tuna Industries in Domestic and Foreign Markets, Report to the Committee on Finance, US Senate on Investigation*

No. 332–313 under Section 332 (g) of Tariff Act of 1930 as Amended, USITC-Publication 2339, Washington, DC: USITC.

US International Trade Commission (1992), *Tuna: Current Issues Affecting the US Industry*, USITC-Publication 2547, Washington, DC: USITC.

US National Marine Fisheries Service (1987), *Environmental Assessment on the Modification to the Marine Mammal Regulations Regarding the Importation of Yellowfin Tuna Caught with Purse Seiners in the Eastern Tropical Pacific Ocean*, NMFS, mimeo.

US National Marine Fisheries Service (1995), *Fisheries of the United States*, Available online: http://www.nmfs.gov (20 January 1996): NMFS.

US National Oceanic and Atmospheric Administration (1997), *El Niño /Southern Oscillation (ENSO)*, Available online: http://nic.fb4 .noaa.gov: 80/products/analysis_monitoring/ensostuff/index.html (16 October 1997): NOAA.

US Congress (1981), *US Public Law PL95-136*, United States Code, Washington, DC: Government Printing Office.

US Congress (1988), *Public Law PL100-711*, United States Code, Washington, DC: Government Printing Office.

Weck-Hannemann, H. (1992), *Politische Ökonomie des Protektionismus*, Frankfurt, New York: Campus.

Wenders, J. (1987), 'On Perfect Rent Dissipation', *American Economic Review*, 77 (3), pp. 456–59.

World Trade Organization (1996), *United States – Standards for Reformulated and Conventional Gasoline – Report of the Panel*, Geneva: WTO.

World Trade Organization (1997a), *EC Measures Concerning Meat and Meat Products (Hormones) – Complaint by the United States – Report of the Panel*, WT/DS26/R/USA, Geneva: WTO.

World Trade Organization (1997b), *United States – Standards for Reformulated and Conventional Gasoline – Report of the Appellate Body*, WT/DS2/AB/R, Geneva: WTO.

World Trade Organization (1998a), *World Trade Organization - Ministerial Declaration*, Available online: http://www.wto.org/wto/anniv/ mindec (22 June 1998), Geneva: WTO.

World Trade Organization (1998b), The Relationship between the Provisions of the Multilateral Trading System and Trade Measures for Environmental Purposes, Including those Pursuant to Multilateral Environmental Agreements, Available online: http://www.wto.org/wto/environ/relation.htm (27 June 1998), Geneva: WTO.

Yandle, B. (1989), *The Political Limits of Environmental Regulation – Tracking the Unicorn*, New York, Westport, CT, London: Quorum Books.

Yang, C. (1995), 'Endogenous Tariff Formation under Representative Democracy: A Probabilistic Voting Model', *American Economic Review*, **85** (4), pp. 956–63.

Young, D. (1990), 'Statement of Rep. Young', in US House of Representatives, Committee on Merchant Marine and Fisheries, Subcommittee on Fisheries and Wildlife Conservation, *Hearing on the International Dolphin Protection Consumer Information Act*, Washington, DC: Government Printing Office, p. 55.

Index